Security of Computer Based Information Systems

Macmillan Computer Science Series

Consulting Editor
Professor F. H. Sumner, University of Manchester

S. T. Allworth, *Introduction to Real-time Software Design*
Ian O. Angell, *A Practical Introduction to Computer Graphics*
R. E. Berry and B. A. E. Meekings, *A Book on C*
G. M. Birtwistle, *Discrete Event Modelling on Simula*
T. B. Boffey, *Graph Theory in Operations Research*
Richard Bornat, *Understanding and Writing Compilers*
J. K. Buckle, *The ICL 2900 Series*
J. K. Buckle, *Software Configuration Management*
J. C. Cluley, *Interfacing to Microprocessors*
Robert Cole, *Computer Communications*
Derek Coleman, *A Structured Programming Approach to Data*
Andrew J. T. Colin, *Fundamentals of Computer Science*
Andrew J. T. Colin, *Programming and Problem-solving in Algol 68*
S. M. Deen, *Principles and Practice of Database Systems*
P. M. Dew and K. R. James, *Introduction to Numerical Computation in
    Pascal*
M. R. M. Dunsmuir and G. J. Davies, *Programming the UNIX System*
K. C. E. Gee, *Introduction to Local Area Computer Networks*
J. B. Gosling, *Design of Arithmetic Units for Digital Computers*
Roger Hutty, *Fortran for Students*
Roger Hutty, *Z80 Assembly Language Programming for Students*
Roland N. Ibbett, *The Architecture of High Performance Computers*
P. Jaulent, *The 68000 – Hardware and Software*
M. J. King and J. P. Pardoe, *Program Design Using JSP – A Practical
    Introduction*
H. Kopetz, *Software Reliability*
E. V. Krishnamurthy, *Introductory Theory of Computer Science*
Graham Lee, *From Hardware to Software: an introduction to computers*
A. M. Lister, *Fundamentals of Operating Systems, third edition*
G. P. McKeown and V. J. Rayward-Smith, *Mathematics for Computing*
Brian Meek, *Fortran, PL/I and the Algols*
Derrick Morris, *An Introduction to System Programming – Based on the
    PDP11*
Derrick Morris and Roland N. Ibbett, *The MU5 Computer System*
C. Queinnec, *LISP*
John Race, *Case Studies in Systems Analysis*
W. P. Salman, O. Tisserand and B. Toulout, *FORTH*
L. E. Scales, *Introduction to Non-Linear Optimization*
P. S. Sell, *Expert Systems – A Practical Introduction*
Colin J. Theaker and Graham R. Brookes, *A Practical Course on
    Operating Systems*
M. J. Usher, *Information Theory for Information Technologists*
B. S. Walker, *Understanding Microprocessors*
Peter J. L. Wallis, *Portable Programming*
I. R. Wilson and A. M. Addyman, *A Practical Introduction to Pascal –
    with BS 6192, second edition*

Security of Computer Based Information Systems

V.P. Lane

Principal Lecturer
Department of Systems and Computing
North East London Polytechnic

MACMILLAN

First published 1985

Published by
MACMILLAN EDUCATION LTD
Houndmills, Basingstoke, Hampshire RG21 2XS
and London
Companies and representatives
throughout the world

Printed in Great Britain by
Camelot Press Ltd,
Southampton

British Library Cataloguing in Publication Data
Lane, V. P.
    Security of computer based information systems.
    —(Macmillan computer science series)
    1. Electronic data processing departments—
    Security measures
    I. Title
    658.4′78   HF5548.2

ISBN 0-333-36436-8
ISBN 0-333-36437-6 Pbk

Contents

v

Preface

Today, computer based information systems play a critical role and integral part in business operations. Companies and governments are involved each day with the electronic transfer of highly sensitive personal data and of data representing billions of pounds. Irrespective of whether or not a company is involved in electronic funds transfer, it is apparent that information is an important and valuable resource of small and medium sized businesses as well as large ones. These and other factors, such as data protection legislation, have combined to raise the subject of security of computer systems and computer based information systems to its current level of concern.

This book presents methods for engineering security into computer based information systems. It is not a computer security handbook because there are good handbooks already written; nor does it try to use checklists to show how to provide better levels of security. Instead, it attempts to show the underlying general principles of security. For example, checklists that are used extensively throughout the computer security industry are not shown in the book, but are discussed and explained as part of other heuristic methods.

A universal problem with books on computer security is that the subject embraces a vast number of topics, including physical security of buildings and computer facilities, fire protection, privacy, software, hardware, personnel management, financial control and audit and the psychological and sociological behaviour of people. As a result, some topics must be left in the background. Also authors may write on the subject from different viewpoints. For example, one author may concentrate on crime incidents, another on database security and another on hardware. My approach is from the educational needs of students aspiring to be systems analysts — an approach that naturally has its own strengths and weaknesses — but clearly this book can give only a broad insight into an extremely complex subject.

Structure of the book

Chapter 1 defines the basic terminology of security of computer based information systems and argues the importance of the subject. Chapter 2 summarises the basic concepts of physical security. Chapter 3 discusses the security of data within the computer and at the man-machine interface through consideration of access control, information flow, inference control in databases and cryptography. The highly specialised subjects of hardware, system software and communications are introduced in chapter 4 but only in so far as they influence computer applications. Chapter 5 explains the critical part played by people in security — people represent both threats and safeguards. In chapter 6 the steps that must be followed to create and build secure application software are examined. Chapter 7 considers operational aspects of security and shows how operational procedures can ensure that well-designed application software does not deteriorate when in operation. Chapter 8 shows how a security programme can be developed for an organisation and stresses the critical role of people — a theme developed earlier in chapter 5. The historical and international background of the UK Data Protection Act with its management, technical and financial implications is reviewed in chapter 9. In chapter 10 the need for both technical and legal deterrents for proprietary software protection is stressed and detailed consideration is given to copyright, trade secret and patent protection. A number of real-life security breaches are described in chapter 11 to highlight points made in earlier parts of the book. One incident is used for a discussion of data protection legislation and the other incidents highlight the importance of contingency planning, company internal controls, recruitment procedures and policies on the use of computer resources by computer centre personnel. The final chapter refers to the need for a holistic approach to security and looks at the security implications of micro-computers.

Suggestions to readers

I have in mind one major group of readers, namely students who in their future careers will design information systems or advise non-computer personnel of a company about security. For these students the book provides a conceptual framework plus an explanation of useful principles and techniques. However, the book should be useful to any reader with a technical background and a serious interest in computing.

To facilitate its use as a textbook, questions are given at the end of each chapter. Pointers to answers are available from the author in a separate document. The majority of questions can be undertaken by a student studying alone, or they can be used for class discussion. There are a few questions, marked 'group problem', which are best studied by three or four students working together.

For the student

The book is intended to serve as a text in computer science or management studies for a senior course at undergraduate level or for postgraduate study. All chapters are appropriate for study but a few chapters — such as those on protection of proprietary software, data protection legislation and the case studies — can be read as separate self-contained studies. The chapters have some overlap but this is intentional because students must appreciate that the many and various security methods complement each other and that no one method can satisfactorily handle the security problems handled by other methods.

The would-be designer needs to appreciate many methods from a number of different chapters. In this sense, the chapters are purely artificial boundaries constructed to help the reader to approach a large subject.

Teaching

Security is not only a fascinating subject in its own right but is also an ideal vehicle to demonstrate the interactions between people and technology in sociotechnical systems. Ideally, the teaching of security should reflect the multi-disciplinary nature of information processing and security. Therefore, it presents a perfect opportunity for team teaching.

Although every effort has been made to eliminate errors, some will inevitably remain. Therefore, I would be grateful to receive comments from readers regarding errors of a typographical or a substantive nature.

Acknowledgements

Figures 1.1 and 1.2 are adapted from figure 7 of block II of the Open University course T301 — Complexity, management and change; applying a systems approach, Open University, 1984

Figure 3.2 is adapted with permission from figures 1a and 1b of the paper 'Data security' by Dorothy Denning and Peter Denning, September 1979, *ACM Computing Surveys*. Copyright 1979, Association for Computing Machinery, Inc.

Figure 8.2 and tables 8.2 and 8.3 are reprinted by permission of the publisher from 'Security risk management in electronic data processing systems' by R. H. Courtney presented at the *AFIPS National Conference 1977*

Figure 8.4 is reprinted from *Systems Thinking and Systems Practice* by Peter Checkland. Copyright (1981) reprinted by permission of John Wiley & Sons, Ltd.

Table 10.4 appeared in 'Computing and reform of copyright protection' by D. J. Grover and R. J. Hart, *Computer Bulletin*, March 1982 and is reprinted with permission of the British Computer Society

Tables 11.1, 11.2 and 11.3 appeared in the *Computer Fraud Survey 1985* and are reprinted with permission of the Controller of Her Majesty's Stationery Office.

Ideas for this book started well before I received the assignment to write it. The interest in security started during the late 1960s when I was data processing manager in the Joseph Lucas Group with responsibility for designing and operating secure payroll and other financial systems. The interest developed over the next decade, first through consultancy assignments in many industries including the financial sector, later through experience of project management of major projects in the public sector and finally through my lecturing in security.

Consequently, I have learned a great deal from many people with whom I have worked and am most grateful to those who have helped directly and indirectly with my work in security. In particular, I would like to thank John Corcoran of National Giro Bank, Frank Davies of Littlewood Mail Order computer services, Mark Kahrs of the Computing Science Research Center, AT & T Bell Laboratories, New Jersey, John Step of the Audit Consortium of the Brighton, Tunbridge Wells, Eastbourne and Hastings Health Authorities and Frank Wright of Southern Water Authority for reading parts of the book and providing helpful comments, and Peri Loucopoulos of UMIST for encouragement during the preparation of the manuscript. I have received help from many colleagues at North East London Polytechnic; in particular Allan Cheatham and John Peacham have commented upon parts of the book, Bill Smith helped with the use of word processors, Joan Mouyia assisted in locating publications and Gloria Shayler produced the artwork. Recognition and thanks are due to several talented and helpful members of the staff of Macmillan. In particular I would like to acknowledge the help of Bill Perry and Malcolm Stewart. Finally, and most important, the support and encouragement of my wife Joan was indispensable.

1 Threats, Safeguards and Security Objectives

Security of computer based information systems is concerned with methods of providing cost effective and operationally effective protection of information systems from undesirable future events. These events, referred to as 'threats', can cause an organisation to suffer a loss and at such times a 'breach of security' is said to have occurred. There are three types of loss, namely (1) loss of integrity, (2) loss of availability of services and (3) loss of confidentiality.

1.1 Security

The rapid growth and widespread acceptance and approval of information technology by organisations have provided many significant benefits, such as better management control leading to increased efficiency at the organisation level. Unfortunately benefits seldom accrue without corresponding undesirable side effects which are often both unforeseen and costly. In this case, there is evidence that organisations are vulnerable to new dangers. For example, information technology has contributed to centralisation of both data and data processing which has created a corresponding and increased danger in the event of fire; but there has also been a major move to distributed computing which has increased the risk of personnel interfering with input and output data. Many organisations are not willing to recognise these threats and although willing to invest significant sums on information technology are unwilling to incur the relatively small additional expenditure to remove or neutralise the threats.

Threats may be caused by

(1) the information system itself — such as communications failure or employee mistake
(2) malicious acts of people
(3) external disasters, such as flood or lightning.

The first of these threats is a major security concern. It requires examination of the performance of an information system to establish that the system performs fundamental critical functions faithfully without undesirable side effects. This aspect of security encompasses reliability of applications, system software, communications, hardware and personnel. People are at the heart of all security safeguards and threats. On the one hand, users, managers, programmers, analysts, operators and many other people design, maintain and operate the security of the system and their contribution to security cannot be over-emphasised. However on the other hand, these same people who are necessarily involved in the information system are often the most vulnerable components of the system. People pose a threat because of (1) accidental acts and (2) deliberate acts. The possibility of inadvertent mistakes by people is fully recognised by designers but the dangers from malicious and deliberate acts receive less attention, except by designers of highly sensitive systems such as those for national security. Although externally created disasters are not common occurrences in a computer centre, few sites are completely immune — for example, from the possibility of extreme weather conditions — and the impact of an external event can be horrendous to an organisation. There are no ideal solutions to the majority of security problems.

With infinite resources it is possible to achieve perfect security but in real terms absolute security cannot be guaranteed even in a technology based subject like computing. The impossibility of perfect security is brought into dramatic perspective by the incident in 1982 of a non-professional interloper breaking the security defences of Buckingham Palace to walk into the bedroom of the Queen, by the American teenage boy in 1983 connecting into the Los Alamos computer and by hackers gaining entry in 1984 to the electronic mailbox service of the Prestel system operated by British Telecom and breaking into client files, including that of the Duke of Edinburgh. Although perfection is not attainable, high levels of protection are possible even with limited resources. Generally, significant security improvements are possible at a cost that is trivial compared with the damage or loss that might be otherwise sustained. Nevertheless, cost is always an important factor in selecting security measures.

1.2 An introduction to security of computer based information systems

An organisation can be considered as a system formed by three subsystems; the operations subsystem, the management subsystem and the information subsystem, as shown in figure 1.1. The operations subsystem encompasses all resources, people and activities concerned with the primary functions of the organisation, whereas the management subsystem includes the resources and activities concerned with the planning, decision taking and controlling of operations. Information, fundamental for the effective operation of modern businesses, is provided by the information subsystem which is an assembly of machines, activities and people gathering and processing data to satisfy information requirements of management, as illustrated in figure 1.2. Consequently, the information subsystem is of prime importance to an organisation and it is worthy of consideration as a system in its own right. Information must be provided quickly and accurately and this can often be achieved only by computer based systems. In the past, computer based information systems supported only the control of the basic operational functions with typical applications being stock management, payroll and management accounting, but their use is now being extended into the management decision making function through the development of decision support and knowledge based systems. As a result, the correct behaviour of computers and information systems combined with accuracy and reliability of electronically provided data are fundamental for the day to day effective functioning of organisations.

In an imperfect world it cannot be expected that information systems will be without fault. Faults may appear in many different forms such as unauthorised disclosure of confidential and sensitive data, risk to national security or loss of money. Security safeguards to minimise the dangers or threats are essential. Unfortunately, information systems vary tremendously in the degree of sensitivity that they represent and the possible threats are correspondingly diverse. Therefore safeguards to neutralise the threats cannot be prescribed in any general manner for an organisation but must be designed for each information system.

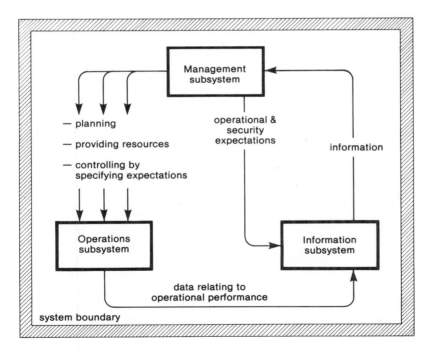

Figure 1.1 An organisation as a system

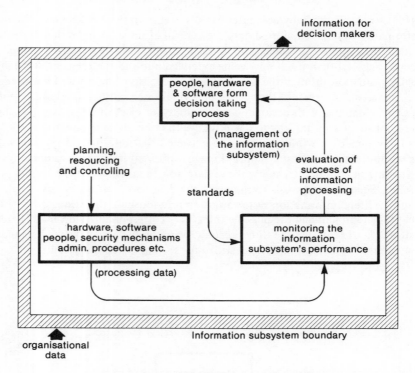

Figure 1.2   Components of an information subsystem

1.3 Breaches of security

There have been numerous reports describing incidents of abuse of computer based information systems, of which a few are considered in chapter 11. Abuse may result in theft of resources within the computer installation, theft of company funds using an information system, illegal access to or use of data, disruption of computing services or theft of proprietary software. Such events are referred to as breaches of security. They are illustrated in table 1.1 and demonstrate that information services can deteriorate through

(1) loss of availability of services (the service is not available at the scheduled time)
(2) loss of integrity (the system does something not intended or does not do something that is intended; or data values are incorrect)
(3) loss of confidentiality (data are revealed to unauthorised people).

Availability and integrity apply to all information systems but confidentiality does not. Security of information systems seeks to eliminate or reduce these risks

Table 1.1   Threats, breaches and countermeasures

Threat	*Loss of*	*Breach of security*	*Countermeasures*
Fire	Availability of computing services	Destruction of data and hardware	Fire and smoke detectors
Insertion of forged input data	Integrity	Financial fraud and corruption of data file	Sound clerical procedures and good administrative practices
Unauthorised perusal of computer reports	Confidentiality	Unauthorised access to sensitive data	Good administrative practices
Unauthorised perusal of terminal screen	Confidentiality	Unauthorised access to sensitive data	Terminal access control
Failure of computer terminal	Availability	Disruption of computing services	A reserve terminal
Noise affecting communications and so data transmission	Integrity and availability	Loss of data	Message sequence numbering
Theft of data file by computer personnel	Availability	Removal and hence non-availability of company data	Vetting of personnel and good operational procedures

of deterioration of services and is a vast subject dealing with hardware, system software, application software, people and organisations. This is not to imply that security has only a technical dimension. It is more than a technical subject and includes the psychological and sociological behaviour of people (Parker, 1981). In fact, the behaviour of people is a major and central factor in security.

1.4 Threats, countermeasures and security functions

A breach of security may be caused by

(1) accidental acts or
(2) deliberate acts.

For example, a fire may be caused by faulty electrics — an accidental act — or by arson — a deliberate act. A good designer attempts to identify such threats to security before they occur as acts, and designs appropriate countermeasures for incorporation within the information system to contain the threats.

Examples of threats, breaches and countermeasures are shown in table 1.1. The steps involved in designing security countermeasures to contain a specific threat are complex and it is a topic that is considered in chapters 2, 3, 4 and 8, but in a more general sense it is the theme of virtually every chapter of this book. For example, the threat of theft of proprietary software and the counter-measures of copyright and patent legislation are evaluated in chapter 10. In all design situations, the analyst must consider the security provided by counter-measures in terms of the following security functions.

(1)	Prevention	This is the ideal theoretical concept which can seldom be achieved because of the cost of constructing or operating the countermeasures.
(2)	Detection	Prevention and detection features are often combined; for example, in the identification and authentication procedure outlined in figure 3.1 unauthorised access is prevented, but in addition all failed access attempts are logged to detect unauthorised activities.
(3)	Deterrence	It is often advantageous to make potential offenders aware of detection and other security procedures because fear of being discovered will prevent intent from becoming violation.
(4)	System recovery	In situations in which prevention, detection and deterrence are not completely effective in dealing with a threat, recovery procedures are necessary; recovery examples are check points in jobs that take a long time to process and backup files.
(5)	System correction	The weaknesses, which caused the need for recovery, must be corrected immediately after recovery.
(6)	Avoidance	It may be the case that in a particular circumstance a specific threat cannot be handled adequately by security countermeasures and therefore the only satisfactory way to proceed is to change the design to remove the threat completely.

In general, accidents caused by human errors and omissions cause more losses than deliberate acts. Therefore, they should be the first to receive attention, especially as a system that accepts a large number of errors provides many opportunities for dishonest activity which can be concealed by the errors. Safeguards that reduce the dangers from accidents contribute to the reduction of opportunities for deliberate acts to abuse systems and to defraud.

1.5 Sensitivity of applications

Information systems are vulnerable to a wide range of hazards (FIPS 65, 1979).

An appreciation of these vulnerabilities is necessary in order to appreciate the problems being addressed in this book. A few typical examples are shown in table 1.2 and it can be seen that the vulnerabilities extend from data input through to errors in the operating system.

Design of security safeguards necessitates the identification of vulnerabilities of each application. However, the weak spots alone are not a sufficient basis for selection of safeguards because the sensitivity of an application is very important (FIPS 73, 1980). The degree of sensitivity of an information system is dependent on the data that it processes and on the way in which the system is used to support other business services. For example, records of monies paid and owed in a finance company are highly sensitive. Examples of systems that may be sensitive

Table 1.2   Vulnerabilities of data in information systems

Area of vulnerability	Example	Type of threat

Input	Data may be altered
	       lost
	       or misinterpreted
		Deliberate
		Accidental
		Accidental

Access	Poor control over who can use a system and who has access to data	Deliberate
	Access is not logged, therefore individuals feel free to peruse data for which they are not accountable	Deliberate
Unprotected data	Data in online files may be poorly protected	Deliberate
	Offline files in libraries may be obtainable quite easily and informally	Deliberate
Undetected errors in programs	Errors in calculations	Accidental
	Subverting programs (Trojan Horse) embedded in apparently genuine programs may allow data to be copied to file areas for use at a later time	Deliberate
Operating system	Flaws in design and/or implementation may allow a user to circumvent controls, erase audit trails or access any data	Deliberate
Controls in application software	Controls in a financial system may be weak allowing a user to (a) introduce false data to defraud (b) introduce erroneous data which affects data integrity	Deliberate Accidental

Table 1.3   Applications that may be sensitive

Type of application	Examples	Security objective
1 Accounting	1.1 Purchases accounting 1.2 Sales accounting 1.3 Payroll 1.4 Stock control	Data integrity
2 General computer processing	2.1 Scheduling of plant maintenance 2.2 Simulation of water distribution network 2.3 CAD	Data integrity
3 Automated decision making	3.1 Reordering of stock 3.2 Automated payments	Meticulous data integrity
4 Management information	4.1 Centralised MIS 4.2 Centralised databases	Data confidentiality and integrity
5 Real-time control	5.1 City road traffic control 5.2 Air traffic control 5.3 Factory automated production control	Continual availability of computer processing and meticulous data integrity
6 Corporate and national systems	6.1 Electronic funds transfer 6.2 Nuclear materials control 6.3 National security 6.4 Car manufacturer's new design	Meticulous data confidentiality and integrity (perhaps with continual processing capability)

are illustrated in table 1.3, but each organisation must examine its own applications to determine the degree of sensitivity that is present.

1.6 Definitions

A number of security terms have been introduced in this chapter. The more important terms are collected together with definitions which are similar to those of the American National Bureau of Standards (FIPS 73, 1980). In later chapters, other terms are introduced and defined as they are used.

Integrity — Data integrity exists when data are the same as in source documents and have not been accidentally or intentionally altered, destroyed or disclosed. System integrity refers to system operation conforming to design specification despite attempts to make it behave incorrectly. Integrity is the guarantee of accuracy, completeness and reliability.

Availability of services — The state when information systems provide services within an acceptable time period.

Confidentiality — A concept that applies to data that must be held in confidence and be protected from unauthorised dissemination.

Privacy — A concept that applies to an individual. The right of each person to determine which data, concerning that person, shall be shared with others.

Vulnerability — A weak point in an information system, allowing the system to be abused and the data or services to be compromised.

Threat — A threat, created by a person or an event, is a potential danger to a component of an information system which as a consequence of the threat may have its functional purpose modified or destroyed.

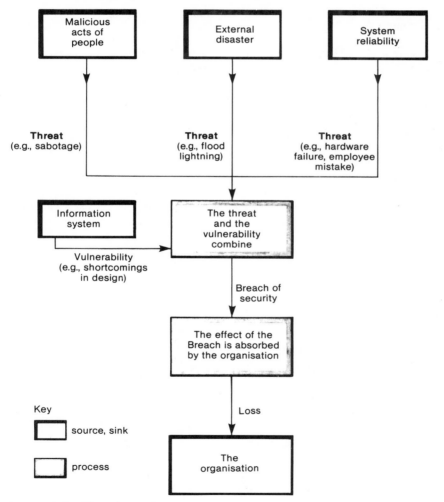

Figure 1.3   The relationships among threats, vulnerabilities, breaches and losses

Loss — The undesirable and end result of a threat such as the added expense of non-availability of services. The relationships between loss and vulnerability and between threat and vulnerability are shown in figure 1.3.

Risk — A quantified assessment of loss.

Protection — A safeguard against loss.

Security — The protection of data from accidental or deliberate threats which might cause unauthorised modification, disclosure or destruction of the data; and the protection of the information system from degradation or non-availability of services.

1.7 Summary

Computer based information systems are essential for the effective operation of modern businesses and, although the financial value of information is extremely difficult to quantify, many businesses have specific information which is so important that its destruction could virtually paralyse the business. Consequently, security is of paramount importance. The need for security is most evident in financial systems but it is fundamental to all systems. Security, a large subject with more than a technological dimension, as illustrated in table 1.4, is complete only if it takes into account the psychological and sociological behaviour of people. Security of computer based information systems deals with managerial procedures and technical safeguards applied to application and system software, hardware, people, organisations and data in order to protect against accidental or intentional unauthorised access to or dissemination of data held in an information system.

Security is an integral part of the design, implementation and operation of an information system. In general, efforts to improve security in an organisation should concentrate on individual systems. An exception occurs when national security is at risk (FIPS 73, 1980). In this special case, there is danger that weaknesses in system software could be exploited to circumvent safeguards built into the application software, and therefore security must be built first into the system software before individual applications are designed. This book deals with security of information systems in the normal business environment.

Since security costs money, there is always need to balance security benefits with cost of implementation. The balance may not always be in favour of security but it is unwise to ignore completely security requirements. Unfortunately they are often ignored because security is a relatively new and difficult problem to many analysts and managers and many of the hazards occur only infrequently. A well-directed security programme will ensure that resources are deployed effectively. This will prevent many threats from developing into security breaches and if a breach should occur the security programme will provide a basis for rapid recovery.

Table 1.4   An outline of security controls

External security control mechanisms	User-computer interface controls	Internal computer controls
Personnel screening	User authentication	Access control
Limiting access to the computer room	Password management	Flow control
Limiting access to computer terminal equipment	Security monitoring	Inference control
Fire protection	Security auditing	Control of data in transit through use of cryptography
Protection against destruction		
Protection against theft of media		

Questions

1.1 Explain the meanings of the terms *threat, vulnerability* and *loss*.

1.2 Explain the meanings of the terms *integrity, confidentiality, security* and *privacy*.

1.3 A new system should have its security aspects open to scrutiny and critical review. Discuss the advantages and disadvantages.

1.4 A member of staff of a company is not authorised to use the computer resources of the company. However he has experience of using computers from his previous employment. On one particular morning when he was not busy with normal duties, he found an unused terminal in another department of the company. Near the terminal was some hard copy from an earlier user. From this he was able to determine the login protocol, the user's name and account number, but not the password. The interloper decided to try to obtain access by guessing the password. After sixty attempts, he gained access with full access rights. He worked at the terminal for one hour and then went for lunch. In the afternoon he returned but found there was no need to login because the machine was still logged on. He made more enquiries and after one hour logged off, gathered his papers together and departed.

Discuss the security weaknesses in the above scenario suggesting improvements where appropriate.

1.5 Identify types of employees within your organisation who could be involved in deliberate attack on your organisation's computer facilities and information systems. Suggest reasons for their behaviour.

1.6 What are the differences between the security requirements of computer based information systems and those of manual systems using clerks and filing cabinets?

2 *Physical Security*

Physical security is a crucial aspect of any complete security plan. It complements the security features provided by hardware, software and administrative and procedural controls. Physical security has a number of different facets — for example, fire protection, building construction and access controls — which can be considered in two major groups

(1) protection against natural disasters like flood and fire
(2) protection against intruders.

2.1 Natural disasters and intruders

Physical security refers to controls and mechanisms within and around the computer centre and remote computer facilities, implemented to protect hardware and data media. As shown in table 2.1 computer facilities are subject to a wide variety of threats because of the nature of the physical environment. The physical environment has a critical bearing on the security of information systems and consequently it is vital to give appropriate thought to factors like building location, design and construction. This should be done early in the planning stage of a computer installation because at this stage security problems are easier to overcome.

Table 2.1   Threats

Source	Example	Type of threat
Natural disasters	Fire Windstorm Lightning Flood	Accidental
Man made	Incompetence Curiosity Civil riots Industrial action	Accidental
Man made	Internal sabotage External sabotage	Deliberate

Table 2.2   Factors that increase vulnerabilities

---

(1) Computer centre equipment is open to staff of many departments of the company and to people from other organisations
(2) Centralisation of computer centre resources at one site
(3) Computer centre located in high risk environment (for example, below flood level, near oil or chemical plant or in high crime area)
(4) High turnover of staff
(5) Low employee morale

It is the organisational environment that creates the specific set of vulnerabilities for a particular installation and, as illustrated in table 2.2, there are many factors that can increase the vulnerabilities.

2.2 Natural disasters

Weather is the greatest natural threat to most locations and there are few sites that are immune from adverse and extreme weather conditions. Wind, rain and storms can have dramatic effects. For example, lightning is unlikely to cause structural damage to modern buildings that are correctly protected but it may disrupt electric power supplies and consequently affect computing services. The effects of floods can be equally damaging but the greatest threat to computer facilities is fire.

2.2.1 Fire hazard and the effect upon site selection

In 1959 a fire in the Pentagon in the USA destroyed equipment and over 7000 magnetic tape reels worth over $6.7 million (AFIPS, 1979). Nowadays, the material used for tapes has been changed from acetate to the less-flammable material Mylar, but magnetic tapes like magnetic disks and paper records are still more vulnerable to fire and more difficult to replace than computer hardware, as illustrated in the case study in section 11.5. However, fire resistant safes are very successful for the protection of media. To overcome the general fire problems, fire precautions are necessary which must (1) prevent a fire from occurring, (2) detect the imminence or presence of a fire and (3) correct the situation with a minimum of damage. A fire safety plan includes

- selection and preparation of site (the prevention function as described in section 1.4)
- detection of fire
- extinguishing the fire
- recovery
- human evacuation of premises.

Table 2.3 Safeguards for fire control

Function of control	*Example*
(1) Preventive	Construction materials for buildings
	Administrative procedures to prevent fire (for example, control of storage of flammable materials)
(2) Detective	Heat and smoke detectors (these controls may activate the corrective device)
(3) Corrective	Sprinkler system using water (water is low cost)
	Gas flooding systems where there is electrical equipment (Halon is expensive but in small quantities is not harmful to people — whereas carbon dioxide is more harmful)
	Training of fire marshals and all personnel
	Clear signposts for exits and fire fighting equipment

Typical safeguards that would result from the operation of this type of plan are shown in table 2.3.

There are two aspects affecting site selection and preparation.

(1) An adjacent check — a check of adjacent buildings and areas adjacent to computing areas. Is there a high risk activity like local storage of paper or chemical processing? The case study of section 11.5 illustrates the type of information that might come out of an adjacent check.
(2) A check of building construction and building materials — some materials are less susceptible to fire than others and some design features, like firewalls, will help contain a fire.

2.2.2 Fire detection

A fire develops through three stages, as shown in table 2.4. First there is smouldering; later the fire develops and flames spread the fire by direct contact; and finally the fire becomes so strong and the temperature so high that the fire spreads by heat radiation. In the last stage heat detectors can expose a fire but by this stage a fire is hard to control. Therefore, smoke detectors are used to attempt to locate fires before they are out of control. To avoid a fire spreading through direct contact, it is necessary to control the storage locations of flammable materials and to complement this control with smoke detectors and heat detectors.

Smoke detectors work on two principles.

(1) The optical scattering principle — which detects smoke because light is scattered by smoke particles. Equipment using this principle will work with the dense white smoke produced by a smouldering PVC cable.

(2) The ionisation chamber principle — equipment using this principle is insensitive to the smoke from smouldering PVC, but it will detect a fire in a waste paper bin before smoke appears.

Detection requires both a combination of heat detectors with smoke detectors and a combination of ionisation chamber detectors with optical scattering detectors.

Table 2.4   Fire development, indicators and detection devices

Stage of fire	Indicator	Detection device
(1) Immediately after ignition	Smoke	Smoke detectors
(2) Spread of fire through direct contact	Smoke	Heat detectors
(3) Spread of fire by heat radiation	Smoke and heat	Heat detectors

2.2.3 Fire control

After a fire is detected, the methods to control it are by using

(1) hand extinguishers
(2) hose systems
(3) automatic gas extinguishers
(4) automatic sprinklers.

Hand extinguishers are a common sight in most buildings but often in an emergency there are few who can operate the equipment. As shown in table 2.5 they do not require the same degree of skill as hose systems but as is the case with all security safeguards it is essential that staff are trained. Hose systems are used by professional fire fighters.

Table 2.5   Skill required to operate fire fighting equipment

Equipment	Operator
Hand extinguishers	Anyone who is trained
Hose Systems	Professionals
Sprinklers	Automatic
Extinguishers using gas	Automatic

Two types of gas system are used — one uses carbon dioxide and the other monobromotrifluoromethane, known as Halon. A gas flooding system fills a computer room with the gas and so puts out the fire. The gas can reach every small void and consequently gas flooding systems are especially useful in confined spaces, such as in a false floor, where other methods have difficulty in reaching. Carbon dioxide and Halon have the advantage that they do not damage computer equipment. Unfortunately, carbon dioxide is harmful to humans. In extinguishing a fire it displaces oxygen. Approximately 30 per cent by volume of carbon dioxide is needed to extinguish a fire in a waste paper bin or one caused by a petrol bomb, but a smaller amount, 10 per cent, renders staff unconscious. Therefore, a carbon dioxide system must not be used before the premises are evacuated. Also, it cannot deal with a fire that rekindles after the gas has been exhausted. A carbon dioxide system must be locked off when personnel are present, and only when premises are unoccupied is it put to automatic. It provides excellent protection because the gas is cheap and extremely effective. For new installations, carbon dioxide systems are no longer recommended because of the danger to humans.

Halon is not so dangerous to personnel because it does not extinguish a fire by replacing the oxygen. It has a chemical action on the combustion process (Hsiao *et al.*, 1979). Halon is more expensive than carbon dioxide and requires a lower concentration to stop the burning process. Irrespective of the gas used, suitable warning notices must be displayed at all entrances to a protected area; also, equipment must only be switched to automatic when people are not present.

Water sprinkler systems are suitable for fighting fires in paper products and building materials but not fires in electrical equipment. A sprinkler system typically consists of pipes which release their water when a valve in the sprinkler heads is activated at approximately 80°C. At this temperature a fire is well advanced and may have caused considerable damage but the main objective of sprinkler systems is to prevent a fire from becoming a major disaster, causing total destruction. Halon extinguishers and water sprinklers are compared in table 2.6.

Table 2.6 Comparison of Halon extinguishers and water sprinklers

Feature	*Halon extinguishers*	*Water sprinklers*
Effectiveness	Very high	Very high
Side effects	Few	Possible water damage to equipment
Recovery	Hours	Minutes if water supply still operates
Operating costs	High	Negligible

2.2.4 Other natural hazards

After fire, the next significant threat to computers is that from water, either as a consequence of a fire or from flooding. If a computer installation must be located in a place susceptible to flooding, some form of waterproofing for the building must be considered. Another consideration in the physical siting of the computer is the adequacy of utilities and protection against their disruption or loss. In particular, electrical power must be continuously reliable and available because computer centres are heavy consumers of electricity.

2.3 Access control and intruders

The fundamental objective of access controls is to allow entry to individuals who have a legitimate need while denying access to all unauthorised parties. If the number of individuals with access to sensitive computer areas is minimised, an intruder must exert considerable effort to enter and is more likely to be seen. A defence plan should establish

(1) physical areas over which control should be exercised as illustrated in figure 2.1
(2) access rights for each specific controlled area for each type of staff and for individuals from other organisations
(3) the methods to be used for control of access.

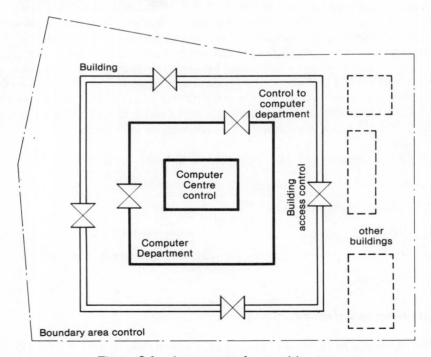

Figure 2.1   Access control to sensitive areas

2.3.1 Sensitive areas

Access controls should apply from the outer perimeter of the computer centre surrounds through to the computer centre itself. As indicated in figure 2.1, protection of the computer centre and its physical surrounds can be considered in four parts

(1) boundary protection which may apply to the area outside the installation building perhaps up to a factory boundary
(2) building access control
(3) computer department access control and
(4) critical area or computer centre access control (AFIPS, 1979; Hsiao *et al.*, 1979)

Although not applicable to office blocks in city centres, a fence around a building or factory perimeter is an important first line of defence. Each possible entry point to the main building should be secured, including doors and other smaller possible entrances like windows and vents for air conditioning. The computer department and centre are critical to the overall security. Therefore they require special protection using a combination of methods such as receptionist control, closed circuit television, guard surveillance, combination or uniquely keyed locks and identification cards and pictures. Access to areas like the tape and disk library will warrant additional controls, as considered in chapter 7.

2.3.2 People with access needs

Once an organisation has established the areas that are sensitive, only personnel whose work requires access on a regular daily basis should be allowed unimpeded access. The movement of all other individuals should be controlled but it is important that clear administrative procedures operate in the control of all individuals with a legitimate need to be in sensitive areas.

2.3.3 Methods for access control

There are three ways of controlling access

(1) by using people, such as receptionists and security officers, as control mechanisms
(2) mechanical devices such as locks and keys
(3) electronic systems such as systems using identity cards and card readers.

A security officer who controls entry to a building or who challenges strangers on their need to enter a restricted area is an example of a method that uses people.

If a receptionist or a security officer is employed in this way, this person must know the procedures to be followed in all eventualities, including allowing access, refusing access and requesting assistance. For general surveillance, a security officer is ideal if the number of strangers is relatively small, but as the number increases the officer performs less satisfactorily. People are an expensive means of detecting unauthorised persons and are better used in overseeing the correct working of other systems.

A basic level of security can be achieved by a simple lock to secure a door. This is a good method of restricting access but it is impracticable where regular and frequent use is needed every day by many people. Mechanical locks are not really suitable unless access is required only a few times each day by each person. For a greater level of security, a room or a building can be controlled and audited through the use of a card reader combined with a lock. The lock is opened by a card containing a mechanical, optical or magnetic code and each card contains a different code number. The system that controls the opening of the lock stores the list of authorised code numbers. The system can be used to allow entry not only by person but also by (1) particular doors, (2) time of day and (3) day of week.

Card systems can have many sophistications. For example, in situations where the highest degree of security is required, the card reader is combined with a push button keyboard and to gain access it is necessary to insert a card into the reader and enter a unique identification code into the keyboard. A card and keyed entry number is somewhat simpler to use than a lock and key entry. Nevertheless it causes inconvenience to staff. If personnel are making numerous entries each day to a restricted area, automatic access control may be advantageous. In this method the device, which is a lock or barrier, is controlled by a signal transmitted by a small electronic transmitter which is carried by authorised parties. Each authorised person collects a transmitter at the start of the working day and retains the transmitter until the end of the day. When a person approaches a restricted area, the electronic system checks whether the person has a transmitter that authorises entry to that particular restricted area. If this is correct the system immediately releases the lock and automatically opens the door. This type of control system is applicable to restricted areas to which access is required frequently by authorised personnel. Many systems incorporate microcomputers which enable complex access control arrangements to be created and operated.

Irrespective of the method selected, the success of a method depends on the attitudes of an organisation's staff and it is the responsibility of management to ensure that personnel realise the reasons for the introduction of access control methods and the contribution personnel must make for the measures to be effective. This topic is considered in detail in chapter 5.

2.4 Conclusion

A systematic approach is necessary if a realistic plan for physical security is to be evolved. However, management must assess exactly what they are trying to prevent and protect, before deciding on physical security measures. This ensures the optimum use of financial resources. To achieve this objective an organisation should

- identify undesirable events
- evaluate physical threats to the computer premises and facilities caused by each of the above events and the probability of occurrence of each event
- estimate possible losses to which the computer premises are exposed
- estimate the annual loss expectancy.

This analysis is referred to as 'risk analysis' which is considered in detail in chapter 8. It provides management with a quantified picture of significant threats from which management is able to assess the relevancy of different security plans by comparing costs with effect on significant threats. This is important because some controls involve considerable financial investment — an example is a Halon fire protection system which costs thousands of pounds — and other controls require a choice between radically different strategies, as in the case of choosing between gas flooding systems and sprinklers.

One of the most difficult problems in security is controlling movement of people, which is the same as controlling access. First, it requires conscious decision making by management, leading to comprehensive, workable and total security procedures. It is insufficient to control most of the people. Control must be total. If an intruder can gain access to the computer room, perhaps after a moderate investment of time and money, without being deterred or challenged, then the company resources that have been expended on physical security have been insufficient, if not wasted, because physical access controls are inadequate. The second point relates to staff acceptance of and commitment to access controls. Access constraints on personnel may cause resentment and affect morale which in turn may influence working efficiency. The successful operation of access controls depends on the commitment and attitudes of an organisation's staff.

Many computer installations develop good physical access controls but then are unwilling to commit further resources for the day-to-day administration and the maintenance of the security controls. To protect against this and to maintain an evolving physical security plan, provision should be made for a periodic audit and critical review of physical security measures. It must be remembered that in some circumstances, physical security measures are the primary means of protection.

Questions

2.1 A computer installation has heat detectors for detection of fire. Discuss the adequacy of this approach.

2.2 In section 1.4 security countermeasures are said to have the following functions.

(1) prevention, (2) detection, (3) deterrence, (4) recovery, (5) correction and (6) avoidance. Discuss physical security in these terms.

2.3 A review of three installations shows that the first uses an old building with a large glass picture window, behind which stands the whole of the installation; the second is in a basement below flood level of a near-by stream, and the third has a picture window, is installed in a basement and has numerous other vulnerabilities. Discuss action that might be taken in each case.

2.4 Complete an adjacent check investigation of your computer centre or any remote site and submit a report of your findings. (Group problem)

2.5 Complete an examination of your computer centre or any other installation with respect to sensitive areas and access control to these areas. Write a report of your findings.

3   Data Security

Data security is concerned with the methods of protection of data in computer and communications systems. In chapter 1, it was shown that security in computer based information systems can be achieved only if there are comprehensive and effective security mechanisms (1) within the computer system, (2) at the user–computer interface and (3) throughout the organisation in which the information system operates. In this chapter, the security mechanisms within the computer system, that is the internal computer controls, are considered. In addition, some of the problems associated with the user–computer interface are discussed because they impinge directly upon data security by undermining internal computer controls that are otherwise perfectly designed.

The computer is the central component of the information system. Equipment manufacturers and software suppliers provide hardware and software features to achieve security within the computer system and at the user–computer interface. Password control and authentication of users regulate entry to the computer system at the interface. Data security is maintained within the computer system by four kinds of control, namely access, flow, inference and cryptographic controls (Denning and Denning, 1979; Denning, 1982).

Access controls govern the objects to which an authorised user may have access. The movement of data from one stored object to another is constrained by flow controls. Statistical databases should not allow a user to extract confidential data through inference. It has been demonstrated by Schlorer (1979) that databases are considerably more vulnerable to this type of attack than many database users appreciate. Therefore, inference controls are essential although they can only reduce the danger and not eliminate it. In situations in which the data are of a critical nature and in need of protection in addition to that provided by other control mechanisms, cryptographic controls may be the only way of providing adequate protection.

3.1 Threats to data

Data in computer systems are in danger from many threats including indiscriminate searching, leakage, inference and accidental destruction as indicated in table 3.1. Indiscriminate searching and scanning of memory and secondary storage is done in the hope of finding software or data that are intended to be concealed and

23

Table 3.1   Threats to data stored in computers and protection mechanisms

Threat to data	*Protection mechanism*
(1) Indiscriminate searching and scanning	Control of access
(2) Leakage	Control of information flow
(3) Inference (especially in statistical databases)	Inference control
(4) Interfering, tinkering or tampering	Access control plus cryptography
(5) Accidental destruction	Access control
(6) Masquerading	Encrypted passwords or digital signatures

Note. In many cases related to threats (2) and (3) the protection mechanisms shown above will be inadequate unless complemented with procedures for recovery

secure. This type of threat is possible only if a user has access to the computer. Therefore, access controls possibly supplemented with cryptographic controls are necessary to neutralise this threat.

A process may have legitimate access to specific objects and then quite improperly release an object to an unauthorised user. This is leakage and could occur, for example, as a result of a compiler leaking a piece of proprietary software during compilation. Information flow controls in support of access controls can ensure that dissemination occurs only to authorised parties.

A statistical database may hold sensitive and confidential data about individuals or organisations. The database is required to provide statistical summaries in response to user queries while maintaining the confidentiality of the information about each individual. A database may inadvertently release confidential information if an interloper poses a series of well-structured contrived queries and correlates the replies to deduce confidential information about a particular individual. Access and flow controls are unable to withstand this type of attack. Protection of confidential data relating to individuals held in statistical databases from this type of attack is extremely difficult to guarantee but inference controls as outlined by Fernandez *et al.* (1981) and Chin and Ozsoyoglu (1980) can help to minimise the threat. Inference controls are feasible but cannot be guaranteed to be effective and they serve only to make the interloper's task more difficult.

3.2 Security at the user–computer interface

3.2.1 Identification, authentication and authorisation of users

Before the internal control mechanisms are actuated, a user must enter a request for access. The object or user must be identified and authenticated before the internal control mechanisms can decide upon the authorisation that that object legitimately has to a protected resource.

The identification of an object, such as a terminal, a program or a user, is the unique name given to that object and by which it is recognised. Identification

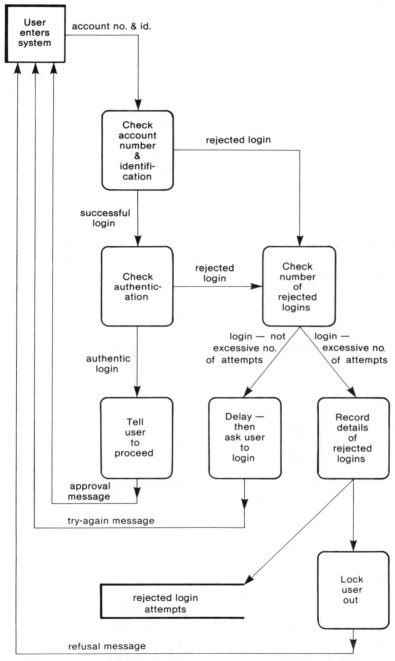

Figure 3.1 A data flow diagram showing an identification and authentication procedure

is the first step in authorisation and is used for accounting purposes. However, identification alone provides little or no security and the critical procedure is the authentication of the identification. Authentication confirms that a person or object is who he, she, or it claims to be. There are several requirements before an identification is accepted as authentic and a typical authentication procedure is illustrated in the data flow diagram of figure 3.1. Except for high-security installations, authentication is normally done only once.

There are three basic approaches to authentication of a user and these employ

(1) a unique characteristic of the person, such as voice or fingerprints
(2) an item that the person has, such as machine readable badges and keys
(3) a procedure that the person knows, such as a password.

The first approach utilises the uniqueness of personal characteristics, and is consequently the most secure, but it is not yet in common use. The second and third approaches are common practice. Badges and keys are used in situations where a high degree of security is desirable, for example in bank computing, and in combination with passwords they can provide excellent protection.

3.2.2 Passwords

This method requires the user to enter a string of characters which the computer checks. If the word entered matches with the password that the computer associates with the person making the entry, access is granted to all the objects authorised for that user.

A simple password scheme might require a user to enter one relatively short string of characters. This is very straightforward for the user and also inexpensive. The user may be allowed to choose the password and in such cases is tempted to select a word that requires little effort to remember but consequently is easy for an intruder to guess. If a less obvious password is selected then the user may consider it appropriate to commit the password to paper which makes it equally vulnerable. The strengths and weaknesses of passwords are discussed comprehensively by Wood (1977, 1980).

If the password is increased in length, it is more secure against the threat of an interloper attempting to discover it by exhaustive search. The time required to break a password is defined by Anderson (1972) and Hoffman (1977) as the expected safe time and is

$$\frac{1}{2} \times (\text{number of possible passwords}) \times (\text{time to enter one password})$$

If the data entry and transmission rate is T characters per minute, the number of characters involved for entry and replying in a login attempt is L characters, the length of the password is x characters, and the number of letters and numerics from which the password is selected is N characters, then the time to break the password is

$(\frac{1}{2} \times N^x) \times (L/T)$

This can be used to obtain an indication of the effectiveness of a selected length of password in a given situation, as illustrated in the following examples.

Example 3.1

Calculate the expected safe time if an exhaustive search is carried out by an operator working at a keyboard.

Assume that the key entry rate T is 120 characters per minute, the character set size N is 20 characters (this means that only a limited set of characters is being used), the password length x is 6 characters, and the number of characters L in the login is 15 characters. Then the expected safe time is

$(\frac{1}{2} \times 20^6) \times (15/120)$ minutes

$= 4 \times 10^6$ minutes $= 7.6$ years

Example 3.2

Calculate the expected safe time if the exhaustive search is aided by the use of a second computer connected to the first computer which uses the password.

Assume that the details are the same as for the example 3.1 except that the two computers are connected by a high-speed line over which the data transmission rate T is 1200 characters per second, then the expected safe time is

$(\frac{1}{2} \times 20^6) \times (15/72000)$ minutes

$= 6667$ minutes $= 4.62$ days

This second example illustrates both the impact of a computer in breaking the password and the necessity to have an automatic delay after each unsuccessful login. This delay is shown in figure 3.1. In this case the delay between each unsuccessful password entry is critical. For example, if a delay of 6 seconds is introduced then the time for each entry increases from 0.0125 second to 6.0125 seconds and the expected safe time becomes greater than 6 years.

The above approach may be extended to calculate a password length to achieve a required performance. For example, if it is assumed that the (required) probability that a correct password will be found by an intruder is p and the time period in months over which systematic attempts are to be made over each 24 hours per day of operation is M, then p will have a lower bound of p_0 where

$$p_0 = \frac{\text{(number of possible attempts to break the password in } M \text{ months)}}{\text{(number of possible passwords)}}$$

The number of possible attempts in M months is $[T(M \times 30 \times 24 \times 60)]/L$. The number of possible passwords is N^x. Therefore

$$p = (4.32 \times 10^4 \times T \times M)/(L \times N^x)$$

The probability that a proper password will be found is p, where $p \geqslant p_0$, which gives Anderson's formula

$$N^x \geqslant (4.32 \times 10^4 \times T \times M)/(L \times p_0)$$

This can be used to select a length of password, x, so that an intruder has a possibility of no greater than p of guessing a valid password as illustrated below

Example 3.3

Calculate the length of a password if 26 characters are used to create a password that will have the probability of not greater than 0.001 of being discovered after systematic attack of one month. The data entry rate is 300 characters per minute and the login entry requires 15 characters.

Using the above equation

$$26^x \geqslant (4.32 \times 10^4 \times 300 \times 1)/(15 \times 0.001)$$

giving

$$26^x \geqslant 8.64 \times 10^8$$

If x is 6 then

$$26^x = 3.09 \times 10^8$$

and if x is 7 then

$$26^x = 8.03 \times 10^9$$

which indicates that a seven character password is required.

From these three examples it is apparent that

(1) the critical factor for preventing an intruder from discovering a password by an exhaustive search, as shown by Anderson (1972), is the length of the password
(2) passwords, even if only five or six characters in length, are relatively safe from systematic attack
(3) passwords will generally not fail because of systematic attack, but as a result of the carelessness of users.

3.2.3 Safer password schemes

There are many variations on the password method which provide better security but cause more difficulty for the user. These include (1) entering only selected characters from the password and (2) one-time passwords. These and other password schemes are discussed in Wood (1980) and their characteristics are summarised in table 3.2.

Table 3.2   Characteristics of authentication methods

Authentication feature	Advantage	Disadvantage
Password selection process		
(1) User selected	Easy to remember	Easy to guess
(2) System generated	Difficult to guess	Difficult to remember
Life of password		
(1) Indefinite	Easy to remember	More vulnerable to exhaustive search; if broken not clear if password has been given away or deduced
(2) Fixed period	Easy to remember and probably safer than indefinite life	Vulnerability depends on the size of the fixed period
(3) One-time use	Prohibits breaking by exhaustive search	More difficult to remember; valid user locked out if exposure occurs
Size of password and character set		
Larger password and larger character sets	More difficult to guess or break	More difficult to remember; may cause the password to be written down
Handshaking		
Dialogues and transformations	More resistant to exhaustive search	More costly and time consuming

In the first method the user is requested to enter only a few selected characters from the password; and the selected characters change at each login. Consequently, an intruder who gains information about one login will have little hope of gaining entry to the system while possessing only a part of the password.

The one-time password scheme is more complex and correspondingly more secure. The user is given a list of passwords, is permitted to use each password once and is required to use the passwords in a pre-determined sequence. For example, if the user has passwords X12, X74, X01 and X11, then after using X12 the user is expected to enter the password X74. Any other entry will be rejected. The main disadvantage of this method is that the user must remember or commit to paper the entire password list and also keep track of the status of passwords. Irrespective of whether a simple or a more complex password scheme is utilised, it is imperative that passwords be protected by the following practical rules which are described in detail in Wood (1980) and Hoffman (1977).

(1) Passwords kept in the computer system must be encrypted.
(2) A password must not be printed on a screen or console, or listed on printed reports. If it is shown, it must be overprinted so that it is illegible to an intruder.
(3) As indicated earlier, the longer the life of a password the greater the possibility of its discovery. Therefore, passwords must be changed frequently in relationship to local circumstances.
(4) The issue of passwords should be through a secure communication channel. For example, it should not be issued at the end of a user session, in case that session is being operated by an intruder.

A password may be used not only to authenticate a user to an operating system, but also for the user to authenticate the computer. To ensure that a user is communicating with the desired computer in a network and not to an intruder in the network, the computer may send a signing-password back to the user. This password will have been agreed beforehand with the user.

3.2.4 Handshaking

An authentication method that provides a higher degree of security than passwords is the handshaking procedure. This may be carried out between two computers or between a user and a computer. In a handshaking scheme the user is given a transform t_u which is known by the computer. For example, when the user wishes to use the system, the computer responds by sending to the user a number y, chosen at random, and asks for a reply. The reply that is required for the handshake to be authentic is $t_u(y)$. If an intruder does obtain values of y and $t_u(y)$, there is still difficulty in deducing the transform t_u. Hoffman states that simple transformations like

$$T(y) = \left[\left(\sum_{i \text{ odd}} \text{digit } i \text{ of } y \right)^{1.5} \right] + (\text{hour of day})$$

increases significantly the effort required to break the scheme. A handshaking procedure is more time consuming to use and is secure only while the secrecy of the transformation itself is maintained.

3.3 Control of access to data

3.3.1 The need for access control

After a subject, for example a user of the computer resources, has been approved as authentic the subject will attempt to access objects. There are user objects such as a file, a record or a program, and there are system objects including files, segments of memory or a protected environment (a domain) in which a process executes. The effectiveness of controls depends on protection of both user and system objects. Therefore, it is essential that each access request be checked to ascertain that the request can be permitted. Approval depends on several factors including

- whether or not the user has been granted the specific access privilege sought
- the access privileges of the terminal through which the user has entered the system
- the operation requested, such as to read or to write
- the datum itself and the value of the datum
- the day or time of the day.

There are two interrelated but separate facets of access controls, namely

(1) the policy which is a specification of the authorised accesses
(2) the mechanisms by which the policy is enforced.

3.3.2 Access matrix and access policy

The access matrix model is a framework for specifying the protection systems in operating systems (Lampson, 1971) and for database security (Conway *et al.*, 1972). The model is defined in terms of

(1) the state of a protection system
(2) the state transitions.

The state of a protection system (Denning and Denning, 1979) may be represented by the triple (S,O,A) where

S   represents the subjects which are the active entities of the model
O   represents the objects which are the passive and protected entities of the system in which each object is identified by its own unique name
A   is the access matrix in which an entry A[s,o] gives the access privileges of a subject s to object o.

In an operating system, objects are entities to which access must be controlled. They include files, auxiliary storage devices, segments of memory, programs and activations of programs. The subjects, including users, processes and domains, are the entities that request access to objects as shown in figure 3.2. Examples of access privileges are execute, read and write. Figure 3.3 illustrates part of an access matrix.

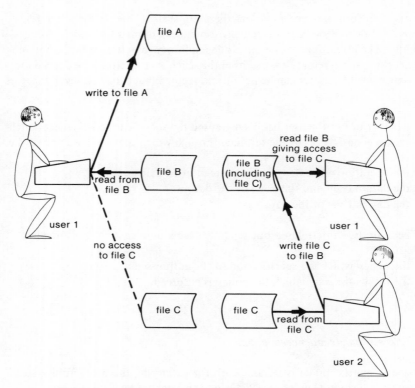

Figure 3.2   Access to and flow of information

	Objects					
Subjects	file 1	memory segment 1	memory segment 2	device 1	subject 1	subject 2
subject 1	own read write	execute read write		seek		call
subject 2		read	execute read write			

Figure 3.3   An access matrix

One approach to database security is to consider it as an extension of operating system security. Thus the objects in the access matrix could be extended to include database items. However, there are important differences between security in an operating system and in a database including the following

- more objects must be protected in a database
- the objects can be complex logical structures (as opposed to real resources in an operating system)
- the lifetime of data in a database is generally longer
- security in a database deals with many levels of granularity such as field, record or file.

Consequently, database security is treated as a responsibility of a database management system rather than the operating system. The database uses the basic security features provided by the operating system and an access matrix as shown in figure 3.4 is developed specifically for database security. The database access matrix is more static than the operating system access matrix. The subjects are end users, groups of users or programs executing at the request of users. The objects are files, relations records or fields within records. Typical access privileges are read, write, update, add and delete. An entry A[s, o] indicates the operations that user s may perform on the data object o and the conditions as to whether or not user s may access the object o. The privileges may be data-independent which are similar to the privileges in operating systems or data-dependent conditions which are related to the values of the data accessed (Hartson and Hsaio, 1975). For example, a user may be permitted to read the salary field of any staff record for which the salary is £15,000 or less, but is not permitted to read the salary if the salary is greater then £15,000. Data-dependent control necessitates a security check being completed each and every time data are requested during processing. This places a significantly greater overhead on the processing than that which results for data-independent access control. The problem can be minimised by input/output routines (Woodward and Hoffman, 1974).

Other restrictions are based upon time-dependent and history-dependent conditions. Examples of these are (1) salary records can only be accessed between the hours of 9 am and 5 pm and (2) a particular user may write to an unclassified file only if the user has not previously read from a file containing classified data.

Subjects	Employee Details					
	name	address	number	qualifications	tel.no.	salary
personnel	read write	read write	read write	read write	read write	read
accountant	read	read	read		read	read write
planner				read		

Figure 3.4   A database access matrix

It is essential to control the procedures that change the access matrix itself. State transitions can be modelled by commands and six basic commands have been proposed, namely to enter a privilege, to delete a privilege, to create a subject or an object and to remove a subject or an object (Harrison *et al.*, 1976).

It must be remembered that the access matrix model does not have to be stored in a matrix form. This would be an inefficient way of storing the model because the access matrix is very sparse and large. The access matrix model is an abstract representation of the security policy.

3.3.3 Access control mechanisms

Design principles for protection mechanisms have been formulated by Saltzer and Schroeder (1975) and include the following.

(1) Least privilege. Every subject should use only the privileges necessary to complete the job. This limits the damage that can result from error or attack and requires that processes should execute in small protected domains. If a default occurs this should lead to immediate lack of access, that is a fail-safe default. Additionally, this principle is a way of containing Trojan Horses — this problem refers to a borrowed program containing undesirable functions not described in its specification (Linden, 1975).

(2) Economy of mechanism. It is better to implement a relatively simple mechanism rather than complicated sophisticated features that are seldom used.

(3) Non-secret design. Security should not depend on the design remaining secret (Baran, 1964). If the system cannot be described safely in open literature, it cannot be used with confidence (this has been explicitly part of the UNIX system since its creation).

(4) Complete mediation. Every request for access must be checked for authorisation. The mechanism must be completely effective otherwise users will find a way of bypassing it.

(5) Separation of privilege. Wherever possible, access to objects should depend on more than one condition being satisfied.

(6) Acceptability. Mechanisms must be easy to use and should be such that it is not significantly more difficult to restrict access to objects than it is to leave access unrestricted.

There are three types of control mechanisms (Denning, 1982) and they are based upon the following concepts

(1) access hierarchies
(2) authorisation lists
(3) capabilities.

User Identification	Privileges
UG07	read, write
UG09	read
US01	read
US02	own, read, write
US03	read

Figure 3.5   A file authorisation list

In access hierarchies, high-ranking subjects are automatically given the privileges of inferior subjects. A supervisor state is an access mechanism based upon this concept. Most systems implement a privileged mode which gives supervisor programs an access domain encompassing every object in the system. A supervisor state does not satisfy the design principle of least privilege because systems programs operate with more privilege than they require for their tasks. Nevertheless, supervisor states have improved the security of many systems at low cost but if a system requires a high level of security then additional mechanisms are essential to limit the access privileges of programs operating a supervisor state.

An authorisation list or access control list is a list of subjects together with the rights of each subject to access specific objects. Therefore, the authorisation list represents the non-empty entries in the access matrix. They are typically used to protect owned objects, for example files. An authorisation list for a file contains the names of authorised users or groups and the privileges of each user, as shown in figure 3.5. Many systems use a degenerated form of authorisation list in which there are only two entries, one giving the rights of the owner and the other specifying the access privileges of all other users. This type of mechanism does not satisfy the design principle of least privilege but a degenerate authorisation list is relatively easy to implement and quite satisfactory in many situations. A legitimate authorisation list can be time consuming to search and therefore many systems do not check the list at every access. Authorisation lists are not appropriate for the protection of segments of memory.

The concept of capabilities is based upon giving permits to subjects. The possession of a permit gives automatic right to the holder to have access to a particular object. The capability is represented in a pair (o,p) which indicates that the holder is unconditionally authorised to have p access privileges to o objects. The concept of capabilities can be implemented at a procedure level and this is consistent with the design principle of least privilege.

3.3.4 Problems with current implementations of access controls

The excessive privilege granted to an operating system is a common and serious problem. The supervisor mode overrides virtually all of the storage protection mechanisms and contravenes the least privilege design principle.

Another problem results from users being forced to pack objects into large memory segments which means that it is not possible to protect individual small memory segments. Hardware is not designed to provide efficient access control because of the overhead of managing small memory segments. Therefore, the ideal of a capability list for each program is difficult to accomplish.

There are other difficulties with access control, including verifying that (1) the implementation satisfies the policy access specification (Gaines and Shapiro, 1978) and (2) the intentions of users are continually consistent with the authorisations permitted (Snyder, 1981).

3.4 Control of flow

3.4.1 Information flow controls to support other control mechanisms

A flow of information occurs from object A to object B if a sequence of instructions is followed that results in information being read from object A and written to object B. The copying of file A to file B, as shown in figure 3.2, is a simple illustration of information flow. Although access controls can be precise about the regulations of accessing objects, the example clearly shows that access control alone cannot regulate the actions that subjects might take with the information contained in the accessed objects. Even with adequate access control mechanisms, information leakage can occur as a result of defective information flow controls. A flow control policy specifies the channels along which information is permitted to flow.

3.4.2 Information flow policy

Typical flow policies specify

(1) two classes of information: confidential and non-confidential objects
(2) a number of authority levels combined with data categories.

In a policy with two classes of information, all information flows are permitted except flows from confidential objects to non-confidential objects.

The second method, that is the multilevel security policy, is often necessary for government and military information. Each security class is represented by a pair (L,C) where L is the authority level and C is the data category. This allows information to be protected hierarchically and by unique disjoint categories (Hartson and Hsiao, 1975). The authority levels might be top secret, secret, confidential and non-confidential and the data categories C1, C2, ... C11, C12. Information flow is permitted from an object with security class (L_x, C_x) to an

Object	Authority Level	Data Categories
x ...... has security class of	confidential	C2, C5, C6, C11, C14
y ...... has security class of	secret	C1, C2, C10
In this case the only permitted information flow from x to y is	confidential	C2
No information flow is permitted from y to x		

Figure 3.6   A multilevel security information flow

object with security class (L_y, C_y) if $L_y \geqslant L_x$ and if the compartments of C_x are also compartments of C_y. This is illustrated in figure 3.6.

3.4.3 Mechanisms for information flow control

Mechanisms can be established to enforce the security policy (a) at execution time by validation of all flows as they occur (Weissman, 1969), or (b) at compile time, verifying all flows caused by a program before they occur, that is before the program executes (Denning and Denning, 1977). The former can be implemented with the access controls of the operating system and requires that a security clearance level be given to each program. Each program is assigned a clearance level which specifies the highest level of memory from which it may read. Similarly, writing to a segment is permissible only if the class of the receiving segment is the same as that assigned to the program. This combination of conditions ensures that the program cannot transmit from a high security class to a lower security class. Unfortunately, it does allow information to move upwards. This problem can be reduced by allowing the clearance level of the running program to start at no clearance and rise, but never fall, according to the highest security level that it has read. This does not eliminate over-classification, because once a specific level has been reached, the level cannot fall again. To enforce precise information flow control, with programs that process different classes of information, more refined hardware and software mechanisms must be used (Fenton, 1974). Nevertheless, extended-access control mechanisms have been used successfully since the late 1960s (Weissman, 1969).

3.4.4 Difficulties with flow controls

Weaknesses of the mechanisms described for the control of information include

(1) over-classifying of information

(2) the difficulty of constructing precise automated filtering procedures for downgrading as a basis for releasing downgraded information

(3) information flows on covert channels (Lampson, 1971).

The extended-access control mechanism does not allow information to flow downwards. Therefore, the only way to regrade data to the correct lower level is by means of a manual override by an authorised person. It is also possible through the use of special programs to downgrade information, but it will be evident from the next section on inference controls that many programs that are thought to filter data to lower levels of confidentiality do not do so.

A program can communicate information to an observer by converting the information into a physical phenomenon. An example is a routine that converts a confidential data value into the running time of a program or other resource usage like page faulting. This type of flow uses covert channels and is extremely difficult to control. One solution requires that each processing job, before it can proceed, must be given an estimate of the resources to be used and the processing time.

3.5 Inference controls

3.5.1 Definition

A medical information system may use a statistical database which is intended to provide health statistics without releasing any information about any one patient. Unfortunately, summary reports contain traces of the original data. An interloper might be able to reconstruct information about one patient by processing and comparing a number of summaries. This is a threat to the person's privacy as a result of deduction of confidential information by inference. Although it may be impossible to negate all inference threats, the aim of inference controls is to make it difficult and too costly for interlopers to extract confidential information.

3.5.2 An example of database compromise

Consider the following dialogue between a user and a medical database.

Question: How many individuals on the database have the following characteristics?

Male	Not married
Height 6 feet	Age 35–40
Weight 182 pounds	
Profession Solicitor	

Answer: 1

Assuming that the intruder, the user, knows the above facts about a Mr Smith, then the intruder can proceed with the dialogue to attempt to find confidential information about Mr Smith. For example, if the list of characteristics in the original question is extended to include one and only one serious disease, then a database reply of '1' indicates that Mr Smith has suffered from that disease or '0' that he has not. The example demonstrates how a resourceful interloper can obtain confidential information from a database. Many researchers have demonstrated the vulnerability of databases and have shown that databases are considerably more suspect than many users realise.

3.5.3 Threats to databases

A statistical database contains records. Some of the attributes of the records are confidential and therefore require protection. If a query is made, the database does not reply with individual attributes but only with statistical summaries about these attributes. Each query is a logical expression using the logical operators. The reply is a set of records that satisfy the requirements of the expression and is called the 'query set'.

Researchers have shown that there are numerous ways of extracting confidential information from a database. Methods of attack that have been identified include those that use

(1) a small query set
(2) a large query set
(3) insertion of dummy records
(4) a tracker
(5) simultaneous equations to analyse the replies.

The example of the medical database security breach in section 3.5.2 is possible because the database reply is a small query set and this permits an individual to be isolated (Hoffman and Miller, 1970). If it is assumed that

the number of people with the property P_q in the query is $N(P_q)$
the number of people $N(C)$ with the properties $P_1, P_2, \ldots P_n$
that is, with the characteristics $C = (P_1 \wedge P_2 \wedge \ldots \wedge P_n)$
is given by

$$N(C) = N(P_1 \wedge P_2 \wedge P_3 \wedge \ldots \wedge P_n)$$

then an individual is isolated if it is known that the individual has properties $P_1, P_2, \ldots P_k$ and

$$N(P_1 \wedge P_2 \wedge \ldots \wedge P_k) = 1$$

A snooper requests the number of people on the database with one property P_x

added to the previous query. If the reply is

$$N(P_1 \wedge P_2 \wedge \ldots \wedge P_k \wedge P_x) = 1$$

then the individual of whom confidential data is sought has the property P_x.

Another attack, which is possible if a small query set is permitted, is to place the individual in a small group with a given property. In this case we do not have a set of properties that uniquely identify the person but know that the individual has i properties. The snooper obtains the reply for i properties, that is

$$N(P_1 \wedge P_2 \wedge \ldots \wedge P_i) > 1$$

Other queries are then posed with p_x property in addition to i properties. If

$$N(P_1 \wedge P_2 \wedge \ldots \wedge P_i \wedge P_x) = N(P_1 \wedge P_2 \wedge \ldots \wedge P_i)$$

then the individual has property P_x.

The above examples indicate that a reply to a database query should be made only if the query set size is greater than an integer, N_{min}. However, restricting the size of permitted replies to greater than N_{min} is not a sufficient safeguard because large query sets close to the database size also allow the database to be compromised. Consider a situation in which there are a large number of people on the file with property P_x and an interloper wishes to discover if a particular individual has the property P_x. If small query sets are not permitted and it is known that the individual is identified uniquely by the characteristics C where

$$C = P_1 \wedge P_2 \wedge \ldots \wedge P_n$$

then the interloper asks for the total number of people with property P_x, that is

$$N_T = N(P_x)$$

If a similar question is posed to give the number of people, excluding the individual for whom confidential information is sought, who possess the property P_x and the reply is N_{T-I} then the individual has the property P_x if

$$(N_T - N_{T-I}) = 1$$

The value of N_{T-I} is found by asking for the number of people with the following properties

$$(\overline{P}_1 \vee \overline{P}_2 \vee \overline{P}_3 \vee \ldots \vee \overline{P}_n) \wedge P_x$$

and the response is N_{T-1}. This is evident from the fact that

$$(\overline{P}_1 \vee \overline{P}_2 \vee \overline{P}_3 \vee \ldots \vee \overline{P}_n) \wedge P_x = \overline{(P_1 \wedge P_2 \wedge \ldots \wedge P_n)} \wedge P_x$$

by de Morgan's law.

If the database management system allows a user to make enquiries and to add records, then it is simple to extract confidential information about an individual who can be identified uniquely by characteristics C. It is assumed that the system will not allow the individual to be isolated because of a protection device on the minimum size of query set. The attack involves entering dummy records of individuals and giving each individual the characteristics C. If the number of records added is at least $(N_{min} - 1)$ then the individual's confidential information can be compromised in the manner described earlier.

A tracker is another attack that overcomes the protection device of query set size. A tracker is an auxiliary expression which produces a reply. This reply is used with other similar replies to deduce the answer for the original unanswerable query. For example, if an individual is identified uniquely by the characteristics C, then this can be represented by

$$C = C_1 \wedge C_2$$

If the system will respond to queries for both (C_1) and $(C_1 \wedge \overline{C_2})$ then $(C_1 \wedge \overline{C_2})$ is called the tracker of the individual (Schlorer, 1975). The example of table 3.3 gives confidential salary details of senior staff in a newspaper business and an interloper wishes to extract the salary of the reporter Ms B. This can be achieved by using C_1 = reporter and C_2 = female so that the tracker is
(reporter $\wedge$ not female) = (reporter and male)

> Question: How many reporters? Answer: 4
> Question: How many (reporter and male)? Answer: 3

These two questions confirm that there is only one female reporter, Ms B.

> Question: Total salaries of reporters? Answer: £68,000
> Question: Total salaries for (reporters and male)? Answer: £48,000

The inference from these answers is that the salary of Ms B is £20,000.

It might appear that it is extremely difficult to compromise a large proportion of the database because of the requirements to know identifying characteristics of individuals in order to build a tracker for that individual. This is not true.

Table 3.3 A database giving salaries

Name	Profession	Male	Female	Salary
Mr A	Editor	Yes	—	£25,000
Ms B	Reporter	—	Yes	£20,000
Mr C	Reporter	Yes	—	£19,000
Mr D	Reporter	Yes	—	£16,000
Mr E	Journalist	Yes	—	£16,000
Ms F	Journalist	—	Yes	£17,000
Ms G	Journalist	—	Yes	£17,000
Mr H	Engineer	Yes	—	£15,000
Ms I	Engineer	—	Yes	£14,000
Mr J	Reporter	Yes	—	£13,000

It has been found (Schlorer, 1979) that trackers are easy to find, perhaps with one or two queries.

The tracker attack takes advantage of the fact that the query sets overlap. The query overlap also allows the database to be attacked by the use of simultaneous equations (Dobkin *et al.*, 1976). If a database consists of a set of numbers, for example x_1, x_2, x_3 and x_4, and it is possible to submit queries about the sum of any subset, then a series of queries and replies can be obtained

Query 1 $(x_1 + x_2 + x_3 \qquad)$ Answer: A_1

Query 2 $(x_1 + x_2 \qquad + x_4)$ Answer: A_2

Query 3 $(x_1 \qquad + x_3 + x_4)$ Answer: A_3

Query 4 $(\qquad x_2 + x_3 + x_4)$ Answer: A_4

The four equations may be solved to find any of the four unknowns, for example

$$x_3 = (A_1 + A_3 + A_4 - 2 \times A_2)/3$$

One way of protecting the database from this type of attack is to ensure that the overlap of query sets is small. If there is no overlap, the database cannot be compromised through the use of simultaneous equations.

3.5.4 Inference control mechanisms and practical difficulties of implementation

The defence mechanisms include

(1) controls on the size of the query set
(2) controls on excessive overlap between query sets
(3) controls that distort the responses by rounding or falsifying replies.

The examples discussed in section 3.5.3 demonstrate that a statistical database is endangered by the presence of either large or small query sets. A mechanism to control size is easy to implement and is valuable. Unfortunately, it is inadequate because it can be subverted by a tracker. A query set control mechanism simply makes the work of the intruder more difficult.

In order to resist attacks that take advantage of the overlap of query sets, that is attacks using trackers or simultaneous equations, it is necessary to inhibit replies to queries where the query sets have too much overlap with query sets of other answers. If enforced, this mechanism may inhibit the replies to genuine and useful queries. Therefore, overlap control is generally impractical because it limits the richness of the database.

The mechanisms discussed above restrict statistics that might lead to disclosure but do provide exact information. Some mechanisms do not provide exact information, but attempt to control disclosure by (1) adding noise to the replies or (2) distorting the values actually in the database. Rounding is a technique that perturbs a statistic before release (Achugbue and Chin, 1979). It is effective with static databases, that is in situations where the user cannot add or delete records. Consequently its application is restricted. Error inoculation (Beck, 1979) distorts the values in the database. This may be undesirable for applications in which the correct data are intended to be available for authorised database users. Sampling is another method that does not give true answers. For replies to queries, only a small part of the whole database is used. The chance of compromise is small because the interloper does not have an opportunity to select the set of records.

The query facilities of many database systems release much more information to the intelligent snooper than many database users have realised. It is evident that the mechanisms discussed above cannot be expected to provide adequate safeguards in many instances. Therefore it is often essential to complement inference controls with threat monitoring (Hoffman, 1977) in which queries are monitored to detect excessively active periods and instances of many successive enquiries using similar queries. Monitoring acts as a psychological deterrent.

3.6 Cryptography

3.6.1 Basic principles and aims of cryptography

In certain situations access, flow and inference controls may be inadequate to guarantee an appropriate degree of protection to information. In such circumstances cryptography may be used to ensure that confidential data, if they fall into the wrong hands, are worthless because the meaning remains hidden. Cryptography, the science of secret writing, has been used by individuals and nations for centuries to prevent access to information in messages (Kahn, 1967). A cryptographic system is illustrated in figure 3.7. A plaintext message M is transformed into ciphertext E(M). This process is encryption. An encryption (or decryption) procedure consists of an algorithm and an encryption key. The algorithm is controlled by the key K. The scrambled message is put into the insecure medium. The receiver uses decryption to recover the message, that is

$$M = D[E(M)]$$

A symmetric cryptosystem uses the same key for encryption and decryption, in contrast to an asymmetric cryptosystem which uses different keys at the ends of the communications channel (Simmons, 1979). Symmetric encryption is the conventional approach and its security is dependent on the key remaining secret. Consequently, the key is communicated from the sender to the receiver along a secure channel which may be slow speed. The scrambled message E(M) is transmitted over an insecure channel.

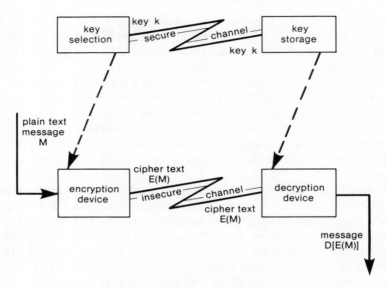

Figure 3.7   A cryptosystem

Encryption mechanisms provide protection in many ways including protection of

(1) passwords
(2) data in databases − in case (a) they are accessed by unauthorised personnel, or (b) a disk containing the database is stolen
(3) information in transit through a communications link, to resist illegal interception by wire-tapping.

3.6.2 Classic cryptographic systems

There are two basic types of cryptosystem, one uses substitution transformations and the other uses transposition transformations. In addition, it is possible to have mixed transformations which combine substitution and transposition. These are referred to as 'product transformations'. The two basic transformations are inadequate for cryptosystems because they are easily broken by the cryptanalyst with the aid of a computer. Product transformations are especially suitable in the computer age.

Substitution transformations take characters in the message and replace them with characters from the cipher code. A simple transformation using a monoalphabetic substitution is illustrated in figure 3.8. In a monoalphabetic substitution a cipher alphabet X is constructed to match the message alphabet A so that each character in A has a corresponding and unique character in X. This type of cryptosystem is easy to break because of many language features (Shannon, 1951). For

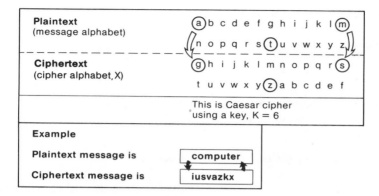

Figure 3.8   A substitution transformation

example, symbols in the ciphertext will have the same relative frequency of occurrence as characters in the plaintext, such as the letter 'e' in the plaintext which will be most frequent. This type of approach can be improved by the use of polyalphabetic substitutions (Kahn, 1967) which hide the language statistical features. In this approach there are a set of n cipher alphabets, x_1, x_2, x_3, x_4, ..., x_n. The first substitution is from x_1, the second substitution from x_2 and so on until the nth character in the message is replaced with a character from x_n. The encryption continues by starting again from x_1. Monoalphabetic or polyalphabetic substitutions can be used with monographic substitutions in which single characters are replaced, or with polygraphic substitutions in which a group of characters is replaced by a similar sized group.

3.6.3 The Data Encryption Standard

The need for a cryptographic standard for government data of a non-military nature was realised by the USA in the mid 1970s. At that time cryptography had evolved since the 1940s only in areas of military and national security. In unclassified government areas there had been little or no development. After four years of careful consideration, the American National Bureau of Standards approved as a federal standard a specific cryptographic transformation, the DES or Data Encryption Standard (FIPS 46, 1977). This standard uses a product transformation of transpositions, substitutions and non-linear operations. They are applied for 16 iterations to each block of the message. The message is split into 64-bit message blocks. After the 16 iterations have been applied to a block, the result is a 64-bit ciphertext block. The key used is 56 bits taken from a 64-bit key which includes 8 parity bits. The DES is illustrated in figure 3.9. The algorithm is used in reverse to decipher each ciphertext block and the same key is used for encryption and decryption.

The DES can be used to support

(1) password protection
(2) end-to-end encryption as illustrated in figure 3.10
(3) encryption of files for storage in removable media.

The DES transformations are suitable for hardware implementation and many DES integrated circuits are manufactured in the USA.

3.6.4 The capacity of the DES to withstand attack

Assuming that the key is unknown, a cryptanalyst has three basic methods of attack.

(1) A ciphertext-only attack — in which the cryptanalyst has copies of ciphertext but does not have or know the corresponding plaintext.
(2) A known-plaintext attack — in which the cryptanalyst has ciphertext and corresponding plaintext.

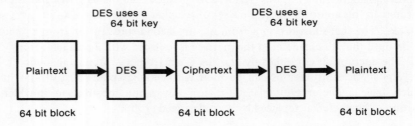

Figure 3.9   The Data Encryption Standard

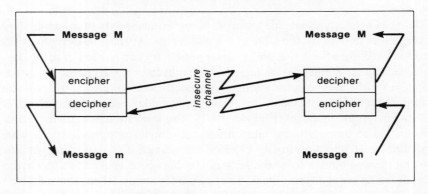

Figure 3.10   End-to-end encryption

(5) The message is recovered from the ciphertext C by calculating

$$C^d \bmod n = M$$

Illustrative example

Consider the simple case in which

step 2a
> the two prime numbers p and q are selected as
> $p = 7$ and $q = 11$

step 2b
> then the two numbers n and r are calculated as
> $n = pq = 7 \times 11 = 77$
> $r = (p - 1)(q - 1) = 6 \times 10 = 60$

step 2c
> select an integer e
> where $e < r$ and
> e has no common factors with r
> take $e = 37$

step 2d
> calculate the integer d
> where $ed = 1 \bmod r = 1 \bmod (p - 1)(q - 1)$
> $37d = 1 \bmod 60$
> $d = 13$

step 2e
> the decryption key, the secret key, is $(13, 77)$
> the encryption key, the public key, is $(37, 77)$

The above example is completely 'unreal' but it demonstrates the process. There are, of course, other combinations of d and e for the values of $n = 77$ and $r = 60$. For example, if e is taken as 11 then a corresponding value of d can be calculated.

In this transformation, the trapdoor information is the factoring of n. There is no proof that factoring is inherently difficult but many mathematicians have tried to find a fast procedure without success. Two European mathematicians have recently developed a fast method for determining if a number is prime (Sullivan, 1982) and it will be interesting to see if this will damage the Rivest public-key transformation.

3.6.7 Digital signatures

Messages that are sent through communications networks may be part of legally binding arrangements or for expending financial resources. Examples are inter-

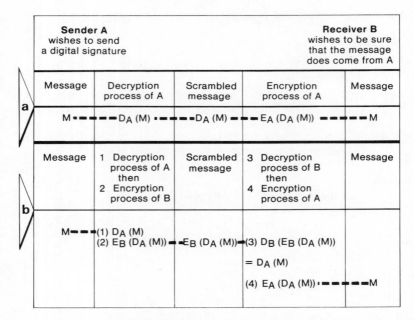

Figure 3.11 Digital signatures (a) without secrecy, (b) with secrecy

bank clearing houses and electronic funds transfer systems. In these situations it is essential to have methods of proving the authenticity and veracity of messages received. In traditional manual systems, signatures authenticate a document. Digital signatures can be implemented by means of a public-key cryptosystem if the cryptosystem has the property $E[D(M)] = M$ which means that encryption reverses decryption. The procedure is shown in figure 3.11. The sender A who wishes to create a signature uses a message M with the secret key K_d for encryption producing a scrambled message $D_A(M)$. Another party B who wishes to check the source of the message need apply only the public key K_e of the sender A to decode the message because only then will $E_A[D_A(M)] = M$. The method can be extended to provide secrecy by the sender A using the receiver's encryption E_B in addition to and after the procedure described above. This method is for secrecy and is shown in figure 3.11.

3.7 Conclusion

Data security is maintained by four kinds of control, namely access, information flow, inference and cryptographic controls. Acting together they reduce, but cannot eliminate, the danger of compromise. All controls have practical and theoretical limitations. Until other forms of personal authentication become cost effective, passwords will remain the normal mechanism for controlling access to remote computing systems. Ideal access control is achieved through application of the principle of minimum privilege and can be implemented at a reasonable cost. There is difficulty in proving that a system actually operates to its access specification and that authorisations are consistent with the requirements of owners.

Flow controls are used with data and with program input-to-output flow to govern the dissemination of information. Mechanisms using security classes can cause information to be over-classified and flows on covert channels are extremely difficult to regulate.

If a user is denied direct access to confidential information in a statistical database, it may be possible to deduce the information by correlating the answers of a number of apparently harmless queries. Inference controls can minimise the leakage but stringent controls reduce the richness of the database. Consequently, flow mechanisms always allow some confidential information out of the database and the control mechanisms are implemented solely to make the intruder's task more difficult.

Cryptographic controls provide protection in situations in which the other controls are inadequate. The security of symmetric cryptosystems is dependent on the safe distribution of keys. Although public-key cryptography removes the distribution weakness there is still a need to protect the central secret key.

There is a wide gap between the protection that can be implemented in a laboratory and that available in many commercial systems. In the context of the total information system, internal computer security is only one component. Most security breaches relate to the external security. Data security is a relatively secure component of the information system.

Questions

3. 1 It is often considered best to permit computer users to have control of their own work. If users are allowed to specify their own passwords why might this be more effective than randomly chosen passwords generated by the computer?

3. 2 Explain why all password schemes are insecure.

3. 3 Calculate the time to break a password system if an exhaustive search is carried out in which the key entry rate is 60 characters per minute, the character set size is 26 characters, the password length is 6 characters and the number of characters for each login is 12 characters.

3. 4 Design a suitable length of password for a situation in which any of 26 characters may be used to create a password that will have a probability of not greater than 0.001 of being discovered after systematic attack over 3 months. The data entry rate is 60 characters per minute and the login entry requires 12 characters.

3. 5 A communications network uses authentication passwords in both directions.

Explain how information can still be intercepted and why the password scheme is insufficient.

3. 6 What are the advantages and disadvantages of

(a) an authentication algorithm compared to a simple password procedure?

(b) a one-time password procedure compared with a simple password scheme?

3. 7 Statistical databases are vulnerable to inference attack. How can threat monitoring help to improve security?

3. 8 Assuming that personal data relating to you are maintained on your college computer, list the properties that would isolate you in a statistical database.

3. 9 A friend is asked to provide personal data which will be kept on a large government statistical database. He does not have to cooperate but he would like to do so. However he is anxious because some of the data provided might be embarrassing to him if the data became common knowledge.

(a) What guarantee should your friend be given if he is to cooperate?

(b) If you are the system designer could you design to these guarantees? Which design areas would be most difficult?

3.10 Your friend in the above question has personal properties p_1, p_2, p_3, and p_4 which identify him uniquely. Write equations to illustrate two ways of discovering if your friend has property p_9.

3.11 It is common practice for passwords to be changed at regular time intervals, for example in universities at the beginning of each academic year or in business computer centres at the end of each month or quarter. Explain the disadvantages of this approach and make proposals for its improvement.

3.12 Explain the differences between *authorisation lists* and a *multilevel security policy*.

3.13 A list of all passwords is kept within an operating system. If a user manages to read the list, password protection is destroyed. Suggest a method that will help avoid this problem.

3.14 Explain why a cryptosystem based on simple substitution is not strong. Are there circumstances in which you would use it?

3.15 Make an appropriate number of visits to the computer centre where your major installation is based, make reference to appropriate manuals and discuss your findings and your queries with senior computer operations staff in order to prepare a report covering the following

(a) manufacturer's security provisions in the hardware and software

(b) passwords and authentication of users

(c) inference control in database software and

(d) cryptography capability.

Your report should take the form of a one page to three page summary of your findings and conclusions. This should have attached to it a number of appendixes showing the detailed results of your investigations, perhaps with one appendix for each of the heads (a) to (d) listed above. (Group problem)

4 The Security Role of Components of Computer Configurations

Control methods for data security are discussed in the previous chapter. They are access control, information control, inference control and cryptography. In this chapter hardware, system software, communications and terminals are considered to show how the four data security control methods are implemented in computer configuration components. Online systems depend for their security on good application software — the design of application software is considered in chapter 6 — but in addition application software for online systems, like other application software, requires a secure environment in which to operate. This environment is provided by the security facilities that are available in and through the components

Table 4.1 Threats related to hardware, communications and operating systems

Type of threat	Threat	Loss
Accidental	Hardware fault	Availability
Accidental	Errors by operators	of
Deliberate	Physical attack or sabotage	services
Accidental	Poor design of man–machine interface	Data integrity
Accidental	Errors by operators	
Deliberate	Unauthorised modification of data	
Deliberate	Unuathorised modification of access tables	System integrity
Deliberate	Unauthorised access by parties masquerading as legitimate users	Confidentiality
Deliberate	Attacks on communications (wiretapping)	
Deliberate	Knowledgeable attacker causes software malfunction to conceal real attack	Confidentiality and data integrity

of the computer configuration. Computer hardware can be arranged to check its own operations and therefore incorporates many and different checks to detect errors. These controls are comprehensive and effective. A decade ago, system software was weak in security terms but today the situation has changed dramatically. Although, it is possible for a knowledgeable person to subvert operating system controls, nowadays the level of security provided in normal systems software supplied by computer manufacturers compares favourably with that within the hardware. The security facilities provided by hardware and software combine to provide a good, although not perfect, foundation on which to build information systems. This is certainly true for centralised and single site configurations. Unfortunately, the situation with respect to multisite configurations, distributed data processing or online systems is less favourable. The complexity compounds the problems of single site operations and as illustrated in table 4.1 may result in errors, omissions and opportunities for the would-be offender.

4.1 Hardware

A computer is a complex electronic device connected to electronic and electro-mechanical input and output devices. Therefore, the threats to which it is subject are (1) machine component malfunction, (2) operator error and (3) deliberate physical attack. Machine malfunctions differ from operator errors and physical attack because they are often not apparent to human observation and therefore require special protection mechanisms. If the hardware components of an information system malfunction, the effect may be a failure of security mechanisms in and around the hardware or elsewhere in the information system. For example, there is the possibility of a hardware malfunction inducing a software malfunction. The major computer hardware components are primary memory, central processing units, secondary memory and peripheral devices. Hardware security is concerned with the building of protection safeguards into these components and arranging the safeguards so that the computer can check its own operations, detect errors and where possible correct errors. The number of safeguards and the sophistication of the mechanisms vary from machine to machine. The variation is influenced by

- the needs of the information system and the user as seen by the designer
- the cost
- the ability of the designer to meet the requirements.

In addition to affecting hardware costs, security devices in the hardware impact upon computer performance. Therefore, hardware protection mechanisms can be considered as an overhead and in the past computer manufacturers have naturally attempted to keep this overhead to a minimum.

The fundamental objective of hardware security is to protect information which is represented in hardware as programs and data. Since the memory units and storage devices are in effect containers of programs and data, security mechanisms are required to

- regulate the transfer of information between containers as considered in chapter 3
- monitor the transfer of information between containers
- create secure containers.

These objectives are achieved by means of (1) memory protection and (2) multiple execution states. However, when implementing these mechanisms the designer of hardware security has the difficulty of selecting an appropriate size of component at which to implement protection. For example, mechanisms for memory protection may be built at word level or at block level — protection at word level is more effective but more costly which illustrates once again the dilemma that the designer always faces, namely that of balancing level of security and cost.

4.1.1 Memory protection

Address space is memory that is used by system and application programs to enable executing programs to make references while completing tasks such as altering the sequence of its instructions or fetching and storing data in memory. There are two types of address space

(1) real memory
(2) virtual memory

and related to each area of memory there is a protection attribute such as read plus write or read only.
    In real memory protection, the memory is partitioned into mutually exclusive areas to which access is controlled. When a program is being executed, the current instruction is held in the instruction register. The central processing unit (CPU) examines the register and determines the memory addresses for carrying out the instruction. Authorised and acceptable memory locations are those that

- have the same protection attributes as the attributes assigned to the executing program
- are confined within the area specified.

If the hardware protection mechanism detects a fault in the memory location or with the protection attributes, the CPU will not complete its interpretation of the instruction, causing a hardware illegal interrupt and the executing program to abort.

Memory protection may be achieved through the use of

- bounds registers
- locks and keys
- access control bits (Hsiao *et al.*, 1979; Peterson and Silberschatz, 1982).

Bounds registers are a set of CPU registers that relate to an area of memory and provide a means of assigning protection attributes to an area of memory and of keeping track of a protected area. Many computer systems use some form of bounds registers where one register indicates the beginning of an area and the other register the length of the area. The CPU uses these two registers to calculate the upper and lower limits of the protected area. A referenced address must lie in these limits or access to the memory is stopped. This simple mechanism is effective but each pair of bounds registers needs an additional attribute register to provide for more effective hardware protection, such as read-only memory.

Memory locks are identification numbers assigned to real memory areas. At any given time, the same specific identification number may be allocated to one or more areas to allow several areas of real memory to be used at that point in time by one executing program, as indicated in figure 4.1. (This contrasts with bounds registers in which executing programs use continuous memory areas.)

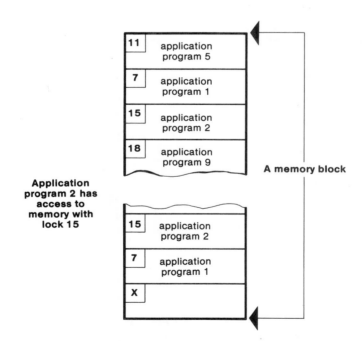

Figure 4.1   Memory protection with locks and keys

For access to be authorised to an area, an application program must provide the key. The advantages of lock and key protection are

(1) different and dispersed areas of memory can be used by one program
(2) a hierarchy of keys can be established — for example, key x might be permitted to open all the locks and no key other than key x is allowed to open lock x where the operating system may possess key x and the operating system resides in real memory area secured with lock x.

The number of locks available to the system relates directly to the number of bits used for identification numbers. If only a small number of bits are used then only a relatively small number of locks are available. In addition, if a large real memory is combined with a small number of locks, then the locked areas are large and the dispersed areas few. This prohibits flexible allocation of memory and protection of small memory areas. One method of overcoming these problems is to use access control bits in which each memory location, say a word, has a tag. A tagged architecture affords a fine-grained memory protection with an overhead cost of extra unusable storage at each memory location.

With protection of real memory, it is difficult to allow different application programs to have different security requirements. For example, in a situation where two programs, referred to as 'subjects' in section 3.3, make access to an object, a common data area

- the first program may be subject to less secure requirements, such as read plus write
- the second program may have stronger constraints placed upon it, such as read only.

Similarly, one program whose key gives it access to two locked memory areas may be regulated by two different protection attributes, for example

- read only for one area
- read plus write for the second area.

These requirements can be accommodated with virtual memory. This provides security over large virtual areas like segments and over smaller areas like pages and parts of pages.

4.1.2 Multiple execution states

It is desirable that system software has overriding rights over other programs. Programs that need these rights are (1) critical programs such as supervisory programs which oversee the execution of other programs and (2) instructions such as input and output instructions whose use is privileged. Since these programs are not necessarily fixed to one area, their protection and the protection of their execution cannot be achieved adequately by memory safeguards alone and therefore additional safeguards are necessary to ensure that an application program is not making privileged instructions. To achieve this, the computer system uses

(1) binary execution states or
(2) multiple execution states

in order to know whether it is executing in a privileged supervisory state or in a non-privileged state.

A binary state architecture, a simple way to create an environment in which overriding rights can be granted, has one state for privileged use and a second for all other use. A program placed in the privileged state may issue privileged instructions but the same code outside the privileged state may not. A multiple states architecture allows programs to have a hierarchy of privileges, for example

- highest level for the supervisor program for software and hardware interrupts
- high level for the supervisor programs for program initiation, termination and accounting
- next level for systems for compilers and editors
- lowest level for the user application programs.

The Multics project is a specialised multiple execution states mechanism which has been implemented with Multics rings in the Honeywell 6000 system (Adleman, 1976). A multiple states architecture has the potential to allow and control the sharing of system resources under conditions of mutual distrust.

4.2 System software

All business applications of computers rely upon a sound foundation of system software. System software, which in general is provided by computer manufacturers, includes compilers and utility programs but in terms of security the most important component is the operating system. An operating system is a comprehensive and complex set of software program modules which enable application software to use the resources of a computer system. It includes

- an executive program, which initiates and terminates application programs, in addition to allocating areas of main memory to the application programs
- an input and output control system, which is activated on request from an application program and causes data to be moved into memory from the communications network or a peripheral unit or to move data in the reverse direction.

Table 4.2   Factors that increase the vulnerability of an operating system

(1) Poor design resulting in the operating system containing many flaws
(2) The operating system is large and complex
(3) The operating system is new and consequently comparatively untried and untested

In addition, it maintains accounts and statistics relating to usage of the computer system, monitors hardware performance to guarantee correctness and cleans up after programs have aborted. The executive program may have associated with it a telecommunications monitor to allow remote terminals or other computers to use application programs or a database management system or both. Therefore over many years, the trend has been to take more of the machine handling tasks out of the control of people and provide for them within the operating system. As a result, on the one hand there has been a reduction in the inherent potential for security breach because of decreased human involvement in operations, and on the other hand there has been an increase in danger because of the possibility of manipulating computer system resources by means of the operating system.

Since the operating system is so powerful, with capability to control all system resources, penetration of the operating system permits access to user areas. Factors that affect the vulnerability of an operating system are shown in table 4.2 but in order to exploit the weaknesses a person must have knowledge, access and motive. Unfortunately, in many computer installations there are knowledgeable software staff who do have these characteristics and can circumvent the controls of the operating system (Scharf, 1980). Consequently, security of operating systems has been an active issue for over a decade.

An operating system that contains flaws in its design or implementation is itself vulnerable and is a weak foundation on which to construct an information system. However a well-designed operating system is a useful, active and essential part of the defences of an information system. In the following section, constituents of an operating system are considered, in order to show how the operating system contributes to the security subsystem of the information subsystem by

- allowing only authorised users and programs to access specific system resources
- preventing accidental or deliberate attempts of aberrant users and programs from trespassing into system areas in which they are not allowed.

4.3 Security functions of an operating system

The functions of an operating system can be classified into two distinct groups, namely

(1) implicit security functions
(2) explicit security functions.

The functions that implicitly relate to security are those that manage and control the system resources and application programs. They include the executive and those routines for scheduling, resource allocation, memory allocation, input/ output and support for communications. The *raison d'être* of these functions is to manage and control the computer hardware resources in order to create a suitable environment for the running of the application programs.

The functions that explicitly relate to security include those provided through devices for

(1) surveillance and identification
(2) access control
(3) isolation.

4.3.1 Management of hardware resources – surveillance

An operating system must be able to identify

- the user
- the resources uniquely.

Resources can be identified by the methods described in section 4.1. In responding to a user, the operating system must

- associate the user with those resources that are authorised for that user
- assign to the resources, during authorisation for a user, appropriate protection attributes such as read only or read plus write
- determine, during program execution when resources are requested, whether the request should be granted or denied – this is done by examining the user identification, the resources requested and the protection attributes assigned to the resources.

In addition to identification procedures, the operating system carries out procedures for

(1) logging
(2) threat monitoring.

If an operating system has granted a request to an executing program, its security work is not completed; it must still monitor the requested operations while they are being completed. For example, if a program is granted access to a statistical database, the program may be allowed access to the data using (a) its own processing routine or (b) a system routine. The latter allows the operating system to control and monitor how the resources are utilised – in situations

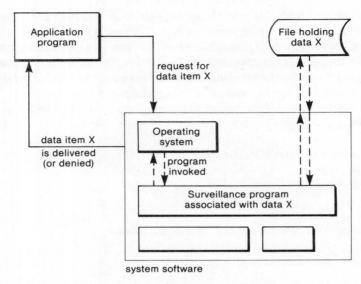

Figure 4.2   Surveillance by the operating system

such as accessing a statistical database this may be critical. As illustrated in figure 4.2, the surveillance or monitoring program may be given wider powers than simple watching, so that it has more effective control. In the case of statistical databases, the powers might include the capability to monitor

- the overlapping characteristics of data from successive enquiries
- the number of enquiries made by a user
- the maximum and minimum values of the data collected.

The significance of these points, related to statistical inference, is explained in chapter 3. To complement threat monitoring, the system software must maintain a log of each batched or interactive processing session. Logging is considered again in chapter 6. Logged data are very important and require special protection.

4.3.2 Access control

An application program that is being executed may

(1) make reference to real or virtual memory — this is handled by the hardware, as already explained
(2) call programs and files — these cannot be handled by the hardware alone and are first handled by the operating system. The operating system manages program and file calls through the use of the access control matrix which is explained in section 3.3.3.

4.3.3 Isolation

Because of multiplicity of requirements, an operating system is extremely complex software and a combination of multiplicity and complexity can result in data spillages and system crashes. Therefore, in the design of operating systems, approaches are practised to partition software and hardware into mutually exclusive compartments, each of which may discharge its tasks in isolation. The objective of isolation is to confine any security breach to the compartment in which it occurs so that no other parts of the system are affected. The basic premise of this approach is that for a similar amount of work one can build a number of independent small systems or a large all-embracing monolithic system; and that it is preferable to build the former because it results in an implemented system which is more secure. Methods that may be used for implementing isolation are

(1) the multiple space method
(2) the virtual machine method
(3) the kernel concept.

In the multiple space method, each group of application programs is run in a separate partition of primary memory; but all application programs are controlled by the same operating system. If a program module is required in separate partitions, then duplicate copies of the module are created in the separate partitions. However, the operating system is not duplicated and the system resources and shared data are monitored by the central operating system. If this method is implemented using multiple virtual spaces, the operating system appears in every virtual space without duplication. The central operating system is the one system and the only system that the computer uses for logging, access and general control, but the complexity of the operating system is not simplified and if the central operating system is penetrated, all the partitions are breached (McPhee, 1974).

In the virtual machine method, which is more common than the multiple space method, each partition may have its own operating system and more than one operating system may exist on the computer system (Weissman, 1975). A virtual machine monitor controls the process. The isolation technique

● is more difficult to penetrate because the monitor program is relatively easier to secure
● allows different operating systems to be used for different security requirements
● removes the danger of one breach of one operating system putting all the other operating systems at risk.

Isolation may also be achieved in other ways. For example, a computer system may be dedicated to a unique set of applications during certain hours of each day or functions may be separated, such as timesharing from batch processing; these are referred to as time-dependent and space-dependent isolation, respectively.

4.4 Verification of software, the kernel concept and penetration tests

If an operating system is conceptually perfect, the question still remains as to whether or not the final physical design matches the initial conceptual design. Verification techniques are used to check the correctness of software (Loeckx and Sieber, 1984). Generally, software specifications are requirement and property statements — rather than procedures to build software — and therefore verification techniques concentrate upon showing that the physical design satisfies the intended requirements. However, verification of the whole operating system may not be possible economically or technically because of the size and complexity of the system. An alternative is to isolate the few functions that are fundamental for the secure operation of the operating system and to collect these functions into a small primitive but complete operating system referred to as the security kernel (Scharf, 1980). The characteristics of the kernel are that it is

(1) complete so that all accesses are checked by the kernel
(2) isolated so that the kernel's code is protected from modification by any other software
(3) correct so that it carries out the functions intended and no other functions.

The underlying idea is to verify the essential parts of the operating system, the kernel, even if the remainder of the system cannot be certified. However, the real difficulty with this approach is that of defining the fundamental functions that form the kernel.

If software is to be certified as secure, it must be provable mathematically. Unfortunately, software verification is extremely difficult and even if verification methods suggest a correct system this does not guarantee a secure operating system. A correct system may be vulnerable because of weaknesses in the original specification. A penetration test may be used to attempt to identify the weaknessess. Knowledgeable and proffesional personnel, who are provided with complete details of the design and the program logic of the operating system, attempt to penetrate the system and so identify weaknesses (Attanasio, 1976). Although penetration tests may give more confidence in the security aspects of an operating system, absolute guarantee is not possible because there may be another penetration test that has not been used.

4.5 Communications

Data communications can be achieved in many ways, for example by mail and courier or by use of the telephone system. In this section, data communications by physical transportation are ignored and discussion concentrates on telecommunications. In the early days of data communications, the volumes of data transmitted were relatively low and included only small amounts of data that were of a sensitive nature; but as telecommunications and computer systems have become more established in businesses, the transmission of sensitive data has become more common. Unfortunately, the transmission methods are subject to

- data interception
- data alteration
- eavesdropping.

Typical data that may be transmitted are those relating to bank accounts and medical records, in other words, data that are sensitive and that must be protected from exposure at all stages of the transmission between originator and recipient. Therefore, a secure communications system is required in which a message is entered by the originator and is delivered

- to the correct output station of the recipient
- with identical content to that which was entered by the originator
- without the possibility that an unauthorised person can delay or learn of the message during transmission.

In a communications environment, many facilities are controlled by third parties, such as the national carrier Telecom, and consequently the user is unable to judge if the services adhere to good security practices. Fortunately, there are many balancing security countermeasures, like cryptography, which can be used to protect sensitive data. In addition, if the public telephone network is used there is less likelihood of penetration at points that are remote from transmission and receiver nodes because of the complexity of the network; and in such cases it is more likely that an interloper will penetrate communications close to terminal equipment since it is at the nodal points that communications lines are easy to identify and interception is possible.

4.5.1 Vulnerabilities, threats and controls

Vulnerability increases in situations where an organisation is highly dependent on data communications. The problem is further increased if there is a mixture of remote job entry, timesharing and transmission between computers or where a distributed computer network uses different hardware suppliers and different protocols.

As indicated in table 4.3 and figure 4.3, threats come from many sources. Even when an authorised user is accessing approved information through the use of an authorised terminal, there is still the danger that data may be lost, copied or corrupted during transmission, especially as telecommunications networks are

Table 4.3   Communications security

Type of threat	Threat	Loss	Security countermeasure
Accidental	Transmission errors; noise; line and modem faults	Data integrity; availability of services	Error detection and correction procedures; fault diagnosis
	Mis-connection (that is, message sent to wrong location)	Confidentiality; interruption to services	Procedures for logging on
Deliberate	Physical attack	Availability of services	Redundancy (for example, alternative line) and physical access controls
Deliberate	Active wiretapping (for example, to change data or to access confidential data)	Confidentiality Data integrity	Encryption, line monitoring and physical access controls
	Passive wiretapping (for example, the monitoring of communications by unauthorised parties)	Confidentiality	

often spread across large geographical areas and consequently are threatened by electrical interference, the weather and human activity. There are three major threats to security of communications, namely

(1) noise which obscures or destroys the meaning of data being transmitted
(2) interception of messages which enables the eavesdropper to obtain confidential information
(3) disconnection which means that services are disrupted and messages delayed or lost.

Security controls that are applicable in the above three situations are error detection codes such as parity checks, cryptography, and redundancy of essential equipment, respectively. Technical breaches of telecommunications are similar to those of operating systems in that they are likely to be carried out by highly skilled individuals. To resist specialist (and non-specialist) intruders, much improvement can be made by the implementation of physical and procedural controls at each communications node. Designers of information systems are usually aware of the advantages of technical methods, such as cryptography, but ignore the benefits inherent in procedural, physical and administrative controls. Nevertheless

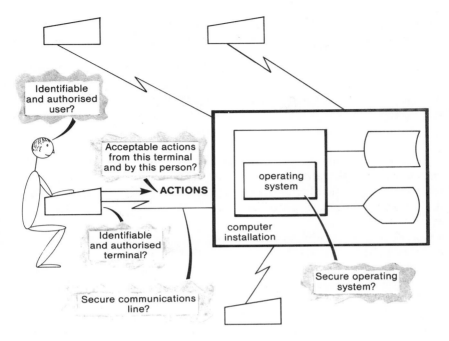

Figure 4.3   Security of computer configurations

in data communications there is always a need for technical security methods in order to achieve reliable and correct message transfer. The methods include communications protocols, transmission modes and data communications software supported by (1) error detection codes like parity checks or polynomial check codes, (2) capability to retransmit, possibly at lower speeds, if message transfer is not completed satisfactorily, (3) alternative transmission routing, (4) a central staff group with responsibility for communications management, monitoring and maintenance, especially if there are many different hardware suppliers and (5) backup or redundancy of essential hardware. These methods are combined to create an effective communications environment in which errors are minimal and errors that do occur are detected and corrected.

4.6 Terminals, distributed data processing and the impact on security of online systems

The service provided in the centralised data processing system of the 1960s was conventional batch processing. The data held by the computer were relatively easy to maintain and the system was accessible only to people who gained access to the computer room. Therefore, security was basically limited to restricting access to legitimate users — although this does not prevent legitimate users from abusing their privilege. Access control consisted of

- a central job control staff unit which took jobs from users so that physical recognition was the basis for identifying legitimate users
- a job submission card with an authorising signature
- a computer operator who had responsibility for receiving and entering work into the system and the processing of each job.

Improvements in computer technology and demands for quicker response times and more distributed services have resulted in application systems changing from batch processing systems to online systems. In online systems computer terminals provide access to computing services using

- a centralised data processing system or
- a distributed data processing system which includes facilities for dispersion of processing capability and facilities like remote batch terminals, direct data entry terminals and a distributed network of computers and databases.

An online system has particular merit because it (1) provides interactive facilities which give direct use of computing services and (2) overcomes the problems of remoteness. Unfortunately, unlike batch processing, an online system does not offer the same possibilities for centralised control over access to the system. An online system may increase the productivity and the effectiveness of the processing service, but it does not necessarily imply security. Irrespective of the form of distributed data processing or whether centralised or distributed processing is used, security is not made easier by the use of terminals. The effect of terminals is to change the scope and nature of the vulnerabilities and the threats.

4.6.1 Terminals — vulnerabilities and threats in online systems

The essence of the problem of protection for an online system is the deficiency or vulnerability of control over the user community. Factors that contribute to increased vulnerability are shown in table 4.4. In many situations these factors combine to pose a serious challenge to security. Typical threats, as illustrated in table 4.5, may result in breaches of security such as

- entry of false transactions, perhaps enabling a person to receive unauthorised payments
- corruption of data files
- use of computing services without payment by a person masquerading as an authorised user
- unauthorised use of computing services as though the computer were a toy.

The problems are compounded by the complex nature of an online system which is dependent on hardware security, operating system security, communications security and identification and authorisation procedures, as illustrated in figure 4.3.

Table 4.4   Factors that increase the vulnerability of online systems

(1) Problems of identification and authentification of legitimate system users
(2) Problems of enforcing security standards on geographically dispersed sites
(3) User has programming capability from remote sites
(4) Sophistication of remote operations (for example, timesharing, remote batch processing and transaction processing)
(5) Weakness of audit trails
(6) Communications lines susceptible to penetration and eavesdropping

Table 4.5   Terminal security

Type of threat	Threat	Loss	Security countermeasure
Accidental	Malfunction of terminal	Data integrity; availability of services	Regular preventative maintenance and backup (that is, extra terminal)
	Human error and omission	Data integrity; availability of services	Training
	Natural hazard	Availability of services	Physical security countermeasures (see chapter 2)
Deliberate	Physical attack causing damage or theft	Availability of services	Physical access controls and redundancy
	Unauthorised use of terminals (resulting in breaches like theft of computer time and files)	Confidentiality; data integrity	Physical access controls, passwords, terminal locks and identification and authorisation procedures
	Unauthorised viewing of data at terminals (resulting in breaches like unauthorised use of confidential data)	Confidentiality; availability of services	Physical access controls, man–machine dialogue and siting of terminals

4.6.2 Controls

There are many techniques and procedures that can be used to minimise the threats to security of remote terminals and online systems. Typical security countermeasures are shown in table 4.5 and discussed below. They include

- physical security
- access control
- protection against terminal malfunction
- administrative controls
- threat monitoring
- isolation techniques.

In a distributed environment, an important task is to secure each remote site. Therefore, where possible the same physical security standards that are applied at the central computer installation should be applied at remote sites. This is not easy because distributed hardware — like small computers, remote batch terminals, and interactive and intelligent terminals — tend to be located in open office areas with minimal physical security. Although many security specialists prefer equipment at remote sites to be behind locked doors, controlled by keys, badge readers, card readers or keyboard entered passwords, it is apparent that there are user advantages in an open office environment. The important point is to have a solid foundation for security which is a management policy that includes for each site (1) identification of person with responsibility for security of the site, (2) identification of persons with authority to use equipment, (3) comprehensive access procedures and user privileges and (4) sanctions that apply if the policy is not followed. Physical security problems are reduced if equipment is isolated from general open office areas and located in separate rooms which can be locked. A further safeguard is to disconnect or disable equipment when it is not in use. It is possible to use advanced surveillance equipment to penetrate a system by picking up electromagnetic radiation from terminal equipment. At present this may not be a significant threat but in the future, as easier methods of system penetration are prevented, electromagnetic radiation surveillance may become more attractive and in such circumstances siting of a terminal room, for example in the centre of a building, is important to neutralise such a threat.

After controlling access to the terminal room, the next requirement is to prevent unauthorised use of the terminal itself or the computing service available through the terminal. To this end, security conscious terminals may be used which have their own hardwired identification and which have built-in readers for magnetic striped cards for user identification. A card entered by a would-be user is read by the terminal and information contained within the card is passed to the computer for authentication. The terminal does not operate if the card is removed from the reader, in addition the user must know and must use the response associated with that particular card. Methods for identification and authentication of users, such as passwords, are fully discussed in chapter 3. However, user identi-fication and authorisation are useless without comprehensive and appropriate physical and administrative controls (Lane and Wright, 1979).

Implementing administrative controls is not easy. The aim is consistent enforcement of security practices and this requires a continuing programme of personnel education in security, as discussed in chapter 5. Each user attends a security orientation course at which the role and importance of each individual in security is stressed and explained. The course complements and is based upon company security policy. The user is instructed in company security standards which should be complete, consistent, enforceable and auditable. Training topics that are of special relevance to terminal users are

- security procedures relating to the handling, storage and disposal of sensitive data and sensitive material
- protection of passwords
- checking the brought forward figures provided by the computer at the start of each terminal session with figures from the end of the previous processing session on the terminal
- logging off the terminal at the end of each processing session and the danger of allowing an unattended terminal to stay online.

Journals or logs will be maintained to provide control; some are manual records, such as those related to terminal breakdown, maintenance and malfunction, and others are generated by the computer, such as threat monitoring logs. Counter-measures against terminal breakdown and malfunction are (1) preventative maintenance and (2) backup terminals. For some terminals a backup machine is imperative but costs are likely to be prohibitive if there is backup for every remote terminal. Obviously, a backup terminal should be installed only in essential cases and therefore each terminal at each site must be judged on its own merits and the decision to provide a backup terminal must be based upon the importance of pro-cessing at that site. The operating system may be used for generating audit logs which are described in chapter 6. Threat monitoring (see section 4.3.1) is another effective safeguard function of the operating system in which the system logs events and if the behaviour of a user appears to pose a threat the user is logged out. It may be advantageous to make personnel aware of the fact that threat monitoring is in operation because its very presence may act as a deterrent. Threat monitoring can check for suspicious patterns of behaviour. An example of this is illustrated in figure 3.1 in which the system counts the number of unsuccessful attempts to gain access and more than a few incorrect password attempts is assumed to indicate an attempt to guess a password.

The methods described above are not intended to be used in every installation or everywhere and at all times in one installation. It is the responsibility of the professional systems designer to implement security countermeasures consistent with the particular needs of each situation. Some situations require the minimum of protection and others require special consideration or special protection. For example, a type of isolation (see section 4.3.3) may be appropriate where (1) certain terminals are used for only specific types of transactions during restricted time periods, (2) certain equipment is used for only certain applications or (3) a closed user group operates which limits the users who may communicate with each other through a communications network and limits the processing permitted.

4.7 Summary

Problems with respect to system software are (1) verifying correctness and (2) incomplete design. These problems are increased if an operating system is large and complex. The operating system for a single site and stand alone computer that is operating in batch mode is much smaller and less complicated than that for a large multiprocessing system with communications to many sites. It is apparent that the size and complexity of an operating system is directly related to its operational environment. As an operating system becomes more complex and as attempts are made to create higher level user interfaces so there is a corresponding increase in security vulnerabilities and the need for more sophisticated and comprehensive protection.

Similarly the complexity of communications, resulting from poling mechanisms, switching equipment and facilities for communications management, increases security vulnerabilities. For example, communications are vulnerable to electromagnetic pickup, jamming and wiretapping. A determined and specialist attacker can use special electronic equipment (1) to emit signals to jam messages and (2) to detect signals that are emitted from terminals as electromagnetic radiation or as noise. In such circumstances special protection is necessary but these are problems of information systems for national security rather than those of normal businesses. With respect to wiretapping, it is difficult to prevent a resolute intruder from finding a place where a line can be tapped, once the intruder has gained access to the premises. Therefore, it is important to have effective physical security measures — like those considered in chapter 2 — to prevent access and so to reduce the possibility of a tap being placed. However, for sensitive data it is necessary to use cryptography.

Distributed data processing and the use of terminals imply user friendly systems and increased effectiveness of computing services, but they do not give greater security since they bypass many physical access controls. This is not intended to imply that online systems cannot be made secure. It is apparent that they can be secure because banks all over the world have installed automatic cash dispensing terminals in public places. The effect of online systems is to change the scope and nature of security threats. For example it is possible in a dial-up computing service for one user to be connected, for this user to be disconnected unintentionally and at the same time for a second user to dial-up and be connected to the first user's session without going through an authentication procedure (AFIPS, 1979).

Entering a system on the back of another user who does not close down correctly — piggy-backing — may be an intentional collusive act, but in most cases it arises simply by accident. It is important that a network is able to positively detect the arrival and departure of users, otherwise port intrusions may occur. A designer must have an appreciation of risks that are inherent in online systems in order to select compensating controls and isolate sensitive areas.

In an installation, a review of security of online systems may be made in two parts. First, the physical and administrative controls should be considered. The second stage is to review the technical controls provided by hardware, communications, software and terminals, but it must be remembered that the technical controls are useless if administrative controls are insubstantial or ineffective. For example, if an intruder has easy access to the computer room and to the operator's console, then the intruder has Pandora's box. Physical and administrative security problems are essentially management problems and not technical ones. With remote terminals, often the prime method of security is a password procedure, perhaps complemented at login time by the use of a device for personal identification. Since password methods are suspect, in the future they will be replaced by identification methods using signatures, fingerprints or voiceprints. In the meantime, while identification techniques are vulnerable and while all systems and all software can be assumed to contain faults, it is imperative to have effective administrative procedures and good application software. These topics are considered in the following chapters and in particular in chapter 6.

Although system software and other technical facilities can be extremely complex and difficult to master, when correctly used they can help to enforce division of duties between staff, limit damage caused by errors, maintain an audit trail, check authorisation and provide many other security aids. However, it is typical and not uncommon for a log of computer use, which is generated by the operating system, to remain untouched and unused. The real problem is that organisations do not exploit the security potential provided by the technology.

Questions

4.1 A company is introducing an online system into a department which has not before used online systems. Discuss controls that could be considered to protect against unlimited access.

4.2 A company locates its computer installation at street level in a room separated from the street pavement by large glass windows. Screens of terminals can be seen by the public. Discuss security implications.

4.3 A company has a large network and is anxious about illegal users gaining access to central resources from terminals at remote sites. Suggest methods for reducing the dangers.

4.4 Select two computers of which you have knowledge and explain for each the method used for (a) hardware memory protection and (b) protection from users of the registers that contain memory protection data.

4.5 In section 1.4 security countermeasures are said to have the following security functions: (1) prevention, (2) detection, (3) deterrence, (4) recovery, (5) correction, (6) avoidance. In terms of these six functions discuss the features of
  (a) hardware
  (b) operating systems
  (c) communications networks and
  (d) terminals and online systems.

4.6 An organisation has only one application out of hundreds that is highly sensitive. It is processed in two hours each week. Discuss how it might be given special protection.

4.7 Discuss the strengths and weaknesses of remote equipment in a distributed data processing environment being located in open office areas.

4.8 Refer to manuals in your computer centre and write a report on (a) hardware security protection and (b) security provided by the operating system of the computer system.

4.9 Visit your computer centre to discover the facilities related to remote terminals and online systems for (a) physical security, (b) access control, (c) terminal malfunction, (d) administrative controls, (e) threat monitoring and (f) isolation. Refer to section 4.6.2. Present your findings in a report. (Group problem)

5   *People and Security*

People are important with respect to security of computer based information systems for three reasons. First, information systems must be protected from people because people can cause threats to an organisation as a result of their accidental or deliberate acts. The second reason relates to the fact that people form components of information systems and therefore may come under threat from others; in this situation protection of people is necessary. Finally, people in their routine work act as security countermeasures.

5.1 The involvement of people in security

Irrespective of the reliability of computers, people will make mistakes, perhaps in using a system or even during the building of hardware. Similarly, the security defences of an information system are designed and constructed by people and as such may contain defects, that is vulnerabilities. It is apparent that in every security situation there is at its core a human activity. Unfortunately, compared with the machine components of a computer based information system, the human components are relatively unreliable and are the most vulnerable aspects of security. A threat created by an employee may be the result of inexperience, incompetence, negligence or malicious acts such as theft and fraud. Consequently, an organisation and its information systems must be protected from people who are inside the organisation and from people who are outside the organisation.

Personnel, like information systems, may be subject to threats in many ways and a threat may cause deterioration of the performance of personnel and of the information systems of which they are components. People can be security countermeasures because of their work. An obvious example is the computer security officer, but all personnel who are responsible for monitoring and control of the day-to-day work with information systems in an organisation may be regarded as security countermeasures. For example, internal auditors and database administrators act as security safeguards while undertaking their routine duties. The situation is illustrated in figure 5.1.

In the following sections, three topics are considered

- protection from people
- protection of people
- people operating as security countermeasures.

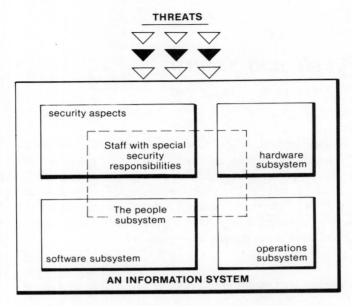

Figure 5.1   People in a computer based information system

5.2 Protection from employees

The human element is present to some degree in all security threats, irrespective of whether the threat is deliberate or accidental. Therefore protection from people is very important. The people who pose a threat may be company employees or people from outside the organisation employed by other companies.

This section deals with those members of an organisation who are involved directly or indirectly with the management, design, development, maintenance, operation and use of computer based information systems, and because of their involvement pose a threat. They include senior and middle managers, systems analysts, programmers, operators and systems users. They pose threats because of accidental acts such as omissions in data at input, overwriting data on disks, coding errors in a program or errors in the system specification and because of intentional acts such as unauthorised browsing through confidential data, unauthorised removal of documents or disks and tapes from the computer installation or inserting a timebomb into a program.

5.2.1 Time-proven long-standing recommended practices

While accepting the fact that the vast majority of company employees are honest and make few mistakes, an organisation must prepare itself against the few employees who might threaten security by deliberate acts. In order to protect themselves, organisations have developed practices that have proven to be extremely effective for maintaining control in manual based information systems. These same practices are also effective in computer based information systems as well as being useful in countering threats from accidental acts (Martin, 1973; FIPS 73, 1980). The recommended practices include the following.

(1) Provision for checks and balances: the checks and balances create a defence which means that a security violation must pass several steps before being successful.
(2) Division of duties or responsibilities: this implies that different personnel are responsible for different steps.
(3) Division of knowledge: knowledge of a system should be divided among a number of individuals.
(4) Job rotation: this implies moving employees from one job to another at random intervals.
(5) Enforced vacations.
(6) Account limitation: an upper limit is placed on the amount of funds that an employee can handle.
(7) Access to information on a need to know basis: Access to information is not based upon rank or precedent but is granted to an individual only if the individual has need and authorisation for access.
(8) Observation by superior: each employee should work under continual observation of a supervisor who knows the employee and therefore may be able to recognise unusual behaviour.

The combination of separation of duties with controls and balances is a long-established concept from the pre-automation era but the combination is an extremely effective technique for reducing risks in computer based systems. For example, the functions of data collection, data preparation, computer operations, systems programming, applications programming, dissemination of output, administration of the database, authorising access to data and internal audit should be separate, with no overlap of responsibility from one function to another. If this type of approach is followed, an employee wishing to break into the system is forced into collusion with employees from a different function; in some cases a system violation may require conspiracy among many parties. An employee is more likely to abuse a system in circumstances where there is no need to have a collaborator.

With systems in which security is of great concern, it is necessary not only to have division of responsibilities but to divide knowledge about the system among many personnel. It is apparent that the role of the systems analyst will often make it virtually impossible to achieve this objective. Therefore, complete division of knowledge should be pursued only in systems containing information of high level security. However, the principle does draw attention to the vulnerability presented by systems manuals and user and programming specifications which are given little protection in many installations.

Vacations contribute to the health of employees but in addition they deter staff from creating a fraudulent scheme that depends on the presence of the employee for its continuity or its secrecy. A scheme of job rotation will have a similar deterrent effect on fraud. In many cases, job rotation is impractical and protection may be dependent on observation by a superior. The case studies presented in section 11.2.2 emphasise dramatically that even a long serving and trusted employee should be subject to continuing observation by a superior.

Irrespective of the success that an organisation has with the implementation of these practices, it must be realised that the practices have limitations. There are always people who must be trusted — for example, the security officer or systems analyst — and therefore there will always be some employees who can compromise security if they wish to do so. Nevertheless, not every employee has to be in a position of trust and in a well-conceived system security will depend on the integrity of only a few personnel.

5.2.2 Good practices developed in the computing industry

The computing industry was quick to realise the benefits of good practices and over a decade ago documentation standards were common. Documentation, guidelines and checklists (Lane and Corcoran, 1978)

- reduce the number of errors and omissions
- contribute to clear communications between one department and another
- minimise the difficulties of program amendment
- ensure operational continuity (a prime objective of security safeguards) in the face of equipment failure and personnel turnover.

Training of personnel is another business activity that the computing industry has recognised as critical. Training to enable personnel to perform normal duties is accepted as the norm, but training in security responsibilities is less common. It cannot be assumed that personnel can actively assist in security without training and management encouragement. Training should cover three areas.

(1) Task training: this includes training in all the skills for specific duties related to security, such as tasks to be undertaken in the case of fire.
(2) Security awareness training: irrespective of whether employees are assigned specific responsibilities for security or not, all personnel should be educated in security topics that include the company's policy on security, data privacy and integrity, the important role that can be played by each employee and the effect of processing delays on the organisation's activities.
(3) Responding to security variances: security variances — such as an unsuccessful

attempt to gain access to the computer or computer room, or a faulty water
sprinkler — occur frequently in organisations. They include any event relating
to security that (a) conflicts with security rules, (b) cannot be explained or
(c) is unusual. If such events are not to be ignored, there must be a procedure
for reporting incidents to a designated individual. Reporting must be in confidence, with no stigma of whistle blowing. The importance of variance
reporting should be stressed in the awareness training, but it must be recognised
that employees will not report all incidents because some incidents will
naturally involve friends and colleagues. Reporting of incidents and the
critical incident technique are considered more extensively in section 8.5.

5.2.3 Systems analysts

Systems staff are in a privileged position because of the nature of their work which
gives them detailed knowledge of many aspects of the operation of their organisation. They have considerable freedom of access and become familiar with staff,
data and procedures throughout the organisation. All these relationships are
essential for system synthesis, for the analyst to build to users' requirements and
to enable the analyst to act as catalyst so that security requirements are built
into the system as described in chapters 6, 7 and 8.

Security must be given careful consideration throughout all stages of the design
process; it must be studied within the preliminary analysis and evolved through
all the development stages, even to the extent of satisfying future needs. The
work of the systems analyst is the foundation for all that follows. Therefore, it
is critical that the work is managed and controlled in a manner to eliminate or
minimise accidental and deliberate threats from the actions of systems analysts
themselves. Typical accidental threats, shown in table 5.1, are caused by the way
in which the analyst carries out design, whereas for deliberate threats the analyst
must be motivated to attempt to breach security. Common motivators are greed
and anger, but other factors can be the cause, such as professional arrogance or
ignorance, as demonstrated in the case study in section 11.3. Motivation or
knowledge of an organisation on its own is insufficient to cause a breach and
there must be supporting circumstances, that is vulnerabilities, before a motivation becomes a threat and before a threat becomes a loss, as illustrated in
figure 5.2. This is the reason why the practices outlined earlier in sections 5.2.1
and 5.2.2 of this chapter are so effective as countermeasures against accidental
and deliberate breaches of security. Three techniques which are relevant for
systems staff are as follows.

(1) Division of duties: a systems analyst is divorced from programming and
    computer operations.
(2) Formal organisational procedures: design work must be authorised by users
    and data processing management and checked by structured walkthroughs

Table 5.1   Motivators, vulnerabilities and threats created during analysis,
            programming and operations

Motivator or cause of act

1. Accidental acts	*2. Accidental and deliberate acts*	*3. Deliberate acts*
Inexperience or lack of expertise	Organisational environment in which analysis is carried	Personal gain
Physical condition, such	out, such as lack of	Anger
as tiredness, overwork	development methodolody	Revenge
Emotional state		Professional arrogance and ignorance

Vulnerabilities

Errors and omissions in design
Poor documentation
Shortcomings in design
Complacency with respect to
designing for security
Working alone or out of normal hours
Poor control over systems staff

Threats

1. Accidental	*2. Deliberate*
Errors and omissions in data input	Browsing through sensitive data
	Sabotage
Overwriting data on backup media	Removal of resources, for example media or programs
	Direct file or program modification

and peer reviews — these procedures will help to uncover errors and omissions
and deter systems staff from specifying fraudulent or disruptive procedures.
(3) Continual and sustained supervision of the analyst by a superior.

5.2.4 Application programmers

The use of division of responsibilities, standards, good documentation and effective
authorisation are as important in programming as they are in analysis and design.
The possibility of errors or omissions passing through development into working
programs must be stopped if at all possible because incorrect programs could
affect all aspects of security, that is integrity, availability and confidentiality.
In this sense, the work of the programmer is more critical than the analyst's
work. Fortunately, the impact of accidental and deliberate threats can be minimised by the use of thorough testing before programs are passed into the production
environment. Testing must be complemented by desk checking, structured walkthroughs and peer reviews.

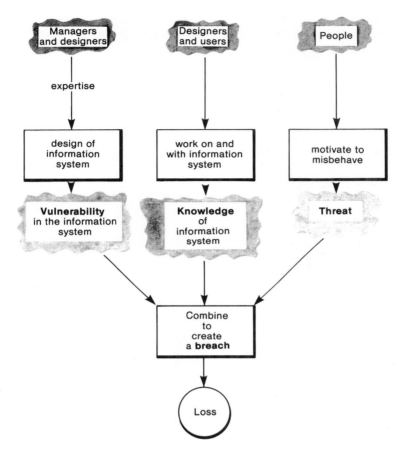

Figure 5.2   The relationship between people and loss

Amendments to programs present a particularly high risk area because they are in a transient state — this topic is considered further in chapters 6 and 8. Amendments present many opportunities for accidental threats. Therefore, strict procedures must be formulated and implemented. For example, amendments should be made to a copy program and testing made with test data under the protection of the operating system to ensure that live programs and data are not corrupted. Senior programming staff have a special responsibility in supervising other programmers and ensuring that all amendment procedures are observed.

In summary there are four principles for the management of programmers involved with systems for which security is important.

(1) Responsibilities should be divided between different programmers so that no single programmer has sufficient knowledge to commit a fraud without risk of being discovered.

(2) Programs should pass to the production environment only after being authorised and approved on a basis of thorough testing, documentation and inspection.
(3) Programmers must not be allowed to have access to sensitive data except under very special circumstances — such as a recovery period after a failure — and while subject to very strict supervision.
(4) Programmers must be aware that their work is monitored and subject to audit (Martin, 1973).

5.2.5 Staff involved in operating systems

The activities in operations are receipt of data, data conversion and processing, production and dissemination of output. Consequently a breach of security can result in loss of data integrity, of confidentiality, or of availability of services. Transient states represent areas of great vulnerability, as explained in chapter 8, and in operations one such situation occurs when data are in transit between departments, possibly even between geographically dispersed sites. In such circumstances the dangers must be recognised and responsibility for data in transit must be placed in the hands of a dependable person for each part of the journey. Other threats with appropriate security countermeasures are shown in table 5.2. Security in operations is considered again in chapter 7.

Table 5.2   Threats and controls in the operations function

Threat	Loss of	Countermeasure
Data corruption through • careless handling of media • malfunction • incorrect processing • double processing	Integrity	Backup copies, journalising, logs, control totals, operating manuals, batch controls
Financial documents (for example, cheques) misplaced or lost	Integrity	Checks and controls (on issue, use, return and accountability)
Misuse of computer resources	Availability of service	Staff supervision and staff not allowed to work in isolation; computer journals and logs
Interface with data • unauthorised viewing by casual observers • obsolete reports fall into wrong hands	Confidentiality	Good operating, supervision, restricted access, output handled by few people All sensitive obsolete output should be shredded

In some installations the actions of computer operators are not constrained and relatively junior staff have responsibility for and access to data that would be subject to tight control by senior staff elsewhere in the organisation. It must be remembered that one operator working unsupervised on the computer can accidentally or deliberately undermine the finest security defences. Powerful system commands, which are discussed in section 11.3, can mask actions of the operator. Therefore, independent control must be exercised over operations personnel because they can influence the system and the audit trail. Control is achieved by a good organisational structure and the use of sound procedures and standards (Squires, 1980).

5.2.6 Users of information systems

In many organisations it is thought that security is only important in and around the computer installation and user departments are not viewed as vulnerabilities requiring protection. This results in an 'iron door' computer installation being built into user departments which are nothing more than 'paper walls'. Users can determine the success or failure of security. As the two case studies in section 11.2 illustrate, user departments can be extremely vulnerable to fraud because users have knowledge of business procedures to make fraudulent practices possible. Consequently, users must be subject to monitoring, control and audit in the same way as are operations staff of the computer installation.

5.2.7 Staff belonging to suppliers

Computer based information systems are dependent on the services of suppliers. Good planning by management can minimise the dangers caused by external staff, as the examples in table 5.3 demonstrate.

5.3 A company policy for recruitment, assessment and termination of employment

Many factors are involved in the protection of information systems from personnel. Nevertheless, statistics show that disgruntled, under-utilised or dishonest personnel account for a large proportion of security breaches. Threats from employees can be minimised by good personnel management based upon sound company policies which include

(1) formalised procedures for recruitment, assessment and termination of employment
(2) a recognition of the effect of staff morale on performance
(3) formal training schemes to promote better performance and security.

Table 5.3   Threats posed by external staff

Service or threat to service	Loss of	Countermeasures
Maintenance of computer and other essential ancillary equipment	Confidentiality of data, availability of services	Controls as for operations staff of host company
Stationery stopped by suppliers • deliberately (for example during industrial action) • accidentally (for example, as a result of flood or fire at suppliers)	Availability of services	Stocks of essential supplies
Electricity supply accidentally stopped by civil engineering contractors, affecting • continuous supply • supply within close tolerances	Availability of services	Special equipment to provide a backup supply a generator an uninterruptable power supply

When recruiting it is wise to apply a vetting process for prospective employees but the success of vetting is highly suspect because virtually all computer security breaches have been committed by first-time offenders. The case studies in chapter 11 illustrate this. During recruitment it is relatively simple to establish the technical suitability of an applicant for an appointment but it is considerably more difficult to establish the suitability of the applicant for the organisation, that is the right person for the job.

Once a person has been recruited, it is necessary to monitor the performance and morale of the employee for the benefit of the employee and consequently for the benefit of the company. In general, all tasks assigned to an individual should be specified in writing. This is possible with information systems because of the availability of comprehensive documentation and procedures such as operating manuals. The employment opportunities must be such that they provide for fulfilment and career development — this is a vital and controversial subject. A poor employment situation, such as under-utilisation of employee expertise, can result in poor performance or even a security breach. For this or other reasons it is inevitable that people will terminate their employment. The organisation must have appropriate procedures to cater for the particular circumstances of the termination — termination of employment is another example of a transient state in which there is high risk of breach of security. Therefore, staff who give notice of resignation must

- be removed from sensitive areas as quickly as possible
- return all valuable security items such as manuals, keys and identification badges
- arrange to cancel and transfer all passwords and authorisations associated with information systems
- undertake to observe the confidentiality of information, such as programs and data, to which they have had access.

It is apparent that proper supervision and enlightened personnel policies after recruitment are as essential as good recruitment methods. Company policy must be such that staff know from the moment they become employees what is expected from them. They must be trained in security task training and security awareness. They must be aware of the disciplinary actions that will be meted out to staff who fail to follow security procedures. Offenders must be disciplined fairly and be seen by other staff to be disciplined.

5.4 Protection of employees

Company personnel are components of information systems and are probably the most vulnerable components. Therefore, an organisation must be concerned with the protection of personnel against damage to health, injury from attack, subversion or blackmail. For example, the data about employees which an organisation holds in personnel records must not fall into the wrong hands owing to lack of concern, because personal records are a potential threat to privacy. There are numerous types of staff involved with the operation, maintenance and design of computer based information systems, including data processing managers, analysts, programmers, operators, users and maintenance engineers. They are valuable and in some cases virtually irreplaceable company assets, and as such it is a management responsibility to create a working environment that protects its employees, for the benefit of both employee and company.

A suitable environment is formed by good conditions of employment and physical security. Good conditions help to reduce sickness, absenteeism, staff turnover and industrial relations problems, leading to fulfilled employees and to more effective information system services. Physical security, considered in chapter 2, includes protection of people from fire, intruders such as saboteurs, explosion (see the case study in section 11.5) and natural disasters resulting from wind, lightning or flood.

5.5 Employees as security safeguards

5.5.1 Senior and middle managers

In the final analysis, responsibility for security rests with top management who must develop and promote

(1) a corporate security strategy
(2) tactical plans to make the strategy a reality.

To achieve this, technical support is required from personnel throughout the organisation. However, there are employees who have special responsibilities related to security because of their work, for example computer security officers, internal auditors, database administrators and middle managers.

Managers in all functions and at all levels should know their subordinates sufficiently well to detect any change in behaviour which might lead to a security breach. Middle managers in particular are instrumental in reacting to security variances and in encouraging staff to report incidents. Middle managers are the cornerstones of day-to-day business operations and therefore of security.

5.5.2 The computer security officer

A large computer installation may employ a full-time computer security officer. The officer reports to user management, monitors and checks to ensure that security procedures are followed and helps to prevent and detect breaches of security. The officer conducts periodic reviews as a cooperative effort and each review is based upon one of the established security checklists which have been developed by national advisory agents (Waring, 1978; AFIPS, 1979). The main role of a computer security officer is not that of an inquisitor but is one of a creator of a secure environment in which employees are aware of their responsibilities and where personnel are not tempted to misbehave, because of their fear of being discovered.

5.5.3 The internal auditor

Security safeguards are simply a special form of control and historically auditors — both internal and external auditors — have been concerned with control. As illustrated in figure 5.3, a control system has mechanisms for

• setting of standards or targets
• recording of performance
• regular comparison of performance with targets
• taking appropriate action to restore activity to desired target.

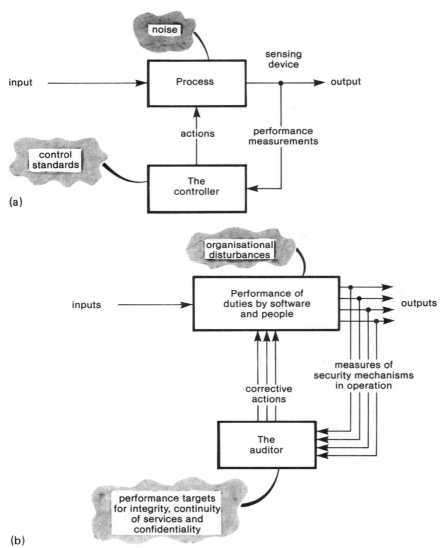

Figure 5.3 (a) Feedback control. (b) The auditor as security controller

In computer security the targets are integrity, availability of services and confidentiality and the auditor (1) reviews, (2) evaluates and (3) reports on security measures to monitor the effectiveness of the security programme. The benefits of using the internal auditor to assist in this work are that auditors

● have an authoritive position, report to top management and are generally free from local or departmental political entanglements

- have wide experience in review work
- have responsibilities that are company wide and consequently encompass information systems.

As a result of organisations now being more dependent on computer based systems, the auditor has had to extend traditional audit methods which had been developed for manual systems and to widen the audit to encompass review during all stages of the development of an information system. The audit includes review of

(1) design and development methods and procedures for new systems
(2) methods and procedures for system modifications
(3) controls to ensure that the theoretical controls satisfy management and legal requirements
(4) controls to ensure that in operation they are reliable
(5) overall control of systems to assess their effectiveness in producing information accurately and punctually.

In summary, the auditor attempts to ensure that adequate security controls are constructed in the system, that there is capability to produce an audit trail during system operations and that time-proven accounting principles are used and complied with in accounting systems.

5.5.4 The database administrator

A database management system presents special problems because the same software is used by a number of different companies and consequently its mode of operation is known to people working with the same software outside the company. It is imperative therefore that outsiders are not allowed access to the organisation. The integration of files belonging to many users creates further problems which require that steps be taken to ensure that

- users have access only to their own data, using rigorous controls, as discussed in chapter 3, such as passwords
- the database is audited regularly (by a database administrator) to secure its integrity
- files and data are categorised for sensitivity
- users have privileges and rights of access on a need to know basis only.

As a result of the complexity of database management systems and their operation, control is essentially the responsibility of one employee, the database administrator, who is fundamental to the efficiency and the security of the operation. The position of power exercised by the administrator is both a weakness and a strength (Watne and Turney, 1984). The post is established to enhance control but the power to monitor activities — such as additions, deletions and changes to the database — may provide the administrator with techniques to subjugate established controls. For example, the administrator may be able to change the database without anyone else knowing, because the administrator is the control mechanism for this activity. These problems of function segregation can be overcome by the practices described in section 5.2.1, namely

(1) job rotation: the person in the role of database administrator is changed regularly and after random periods
(2) supervision by superior
(3) journalising: requests by the administrator for access to the database are logged for later examination by the auditor for unauthorised activities.

5.6 Summary

People are the mainspring or play a major part in all security vulnerabilities. The vulnerability of information systems can permit accidental or deliberate acts to cause security losses. All information systems need protection to some degree from people. This is achieved by comprehensive and substantive controls. Often it is advantageous for employees to know of security countermeasures as well as their own contribution and that of their colleagues in creating a secure environment, because if the defences are good, a potential offender is deterred.

Certain employees are essential components of information systems and therefore need protection like any other system components. Irrespective of how successful an organisation is in establishing procedures to protect (1) its systems from employees and (2) its employees, there is always need to put trust in key personnel who, if they wish to do so, can compromise security. Key personnel include systems analysts and also people who have a special security responsibility in that they are themselves security countermeasures. Not every employee needs to be in a position of trust and in a well-regulated organisation there will be few people whose work is not subject to some form of security control.

Questions

5.1 Identify people outside your college or organisation who pose a threat to computer based information systems and therefore to the organisation. Explain why they pose a threat and the safeguards that can be used against these threats.

5.2 Explain how the principle of division of duties helps to ensure the integrity of a financial transaction within an information system.

5.3 It would appear to be advantageous to employ computer operators who have no knowledge of programming. Discuss.

5.4 Job rotation has many disadvantages. Discuss.

5.5 To comply with the objective of division of knowledge it is necessary that each development project should have at least two systems analysts. Discuss.

5.6 Analyse the two case studies in section 11.2 to show which good practices were not in operation.

5.7 The protection of personnel requires good conditions of employment. Explain what is meant by 'good conditions' and discuss the relevance of this to security.

5.8 The internal auditor needs to review only the controls that exist in current systems and not waste time considering methods used in the development of new systems. Discuss.

5.9 (a) List the tasks that are the responsibilities of the computer security officer.

    (b) In a small installation with say 2 or 3 programmer/analysts
        (1) who undertakes these responsibilities?
        (2) are there any duties of the security officer not applicable to this situation?

5.10 Two computer security officers have each served their respective organisations for ten years. The two officers have applied for a job with your organisation and they appear very similar in age, qualifications, experience, references and resourcefulness. The only real difference is that the first officer, CSO1, throughout his ten years has continually discovered computer personnel and users taking advantage of their employment to the disadvantage of their employer; whereas CSO2 had in ten years discovered only two breaches, one major and one minor – in the case of the minor offence the CSO2 had recommended that the party be warned but kept with the company – in the major incident, the employee was dismissed without any charges being brought.

    Your personnel officer recommends that the second computer security officer be offered the appointment. Explain

    (a) reasons why the first security officer might be preferred

    (b) the reasoning of the personnel officer.

5.11 What methods can be used to ensure that the work of an applications programmer is secure? Indicate key areas for control of applications programmers.

5.12 In the final analysis, security depends upon the honesty of people. Therefore, an organisation should concentrate on sound recruitment procedures; then the technical and administrative security procedures that are recommended for employee control can be ignored, which is just as well because they never guarantee security. Discuss.

5.13 Discuss the safeguards that can be used to help reduce the danger of un-
scrupulous programmers constructing vulnerabilities in programs.

6 Implementing Security Controls in Application Software During the Design and Build Phases

This chapter considers the steps that should be taken to ensure that security measures are incorporated into the application software during the design and build stages. In this process, responsibility for security policy lies with management of the organisation, with system users and with internal auditors, but the actual detailed design and implementation of security measures may be delegated to system designers.

6.1 Management, users and security safeguards

Components of an information system include people who use the system, technical staff who operate the system, hardware and system software. Another major component is the application software, formed by the computer programs which are at the centre of the information system. For the application software to operate effectively, security mechanisms and controls are necessary within the software and at the interface between the software and other components of the information system. The safeguards may vary from sophisticated technical controls to simple and common reconciliation controls. Each type of safeguard has its place and it is well to remember that there are few reported cases of breach of hardware protection but many incidents relating to individuals bypassing administrative controls to penetrate a system without the technical controls being able to compensate. Security must be comprehensive and also an integral part of both development and operation of the system. In chapter 1 and in table 6.1, it is shown that different systems have different security needs. Therefore, the security measures implemented must reflect the needs of that system and be consistent with the sensitivity of the data processed by the system and with the support given by the system to business activities.

The objective of good design is to build application software that is secure. This demands a systematic approach to design which takes into account the organisational environment in which the design takes place and which covers planning of development, design methods and selection of security mechanisms. The process involves many personnel, including management, system users and auditors as well as professional computer staff. Therefore, in the following sections consideration is given to (1) the organisation in which design occurs, before attention is turned to (2) a security design methodology and (3) the basic controls that can be placed at the interface of or within the application software. The relationships among these three security areas are illustrated in figure 6.1.

Table 6.1 Threats and typical information systems

Information system		Major threat	Major security objective
type	examples		
(1) Financial and asset management	Payroll, stock management and purchase accounts	Deliberate and accidental acts	Integrity
(2) Processing in support of business operations	CAD and medical support	Accidental acts	Integrity
(3) Automated decision making	Stock recording and maintenance scheduling	Accidental acts	Rigorous integrity

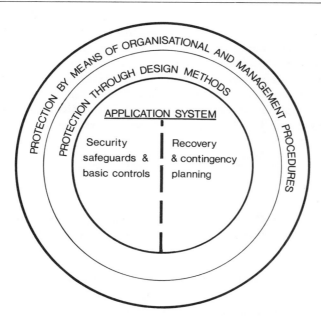

Figure 6.1 Security safeguards provided through design methods, organisational procedures and application software

6.2 The management and organisational environment

Selection of security controls depends on more than sensitivity of data processed and contribution of the system to business activities. Vulnerabilities that arise in the infrastructure in which the system operates have a major influence on the security selection and system operational effectiveness. There are numerous organisational factors which shape the environment in which the information systems operate including

- company security policy
- management procedures used for the control of development of information systems
- the use of time-honoured personnel aspects of control.

An information system can be secure only if it is part of an organisation with a positive attitude to security. An organisation should have a working policy covering internal and external security so that members of staff know their responsibility for preventing data being passed to unauthorised parties (Squires, 1980). Similarly, an organisation should endeavour to create a sound project management environment for systems development. Project management will provide a solid framework for design, to which security safeguards can be added relatively easily.

Organisations should ensure that in information systems, and in the business in general, time-honoured personnel practices are used. Some of these practices were described in chapter 5 including the practices of segregation of duties, job rotation and limitation of access; associated procedures for employment and termination of contract; and the principle that all work must be supervised (FIPS 73, 1980). The way these practices are used will depend not only on the information system but also on the characteristics of the organisation. For example, a small organisation may find it virtually impossible to implement all the practices because of cost.

6.3 Design methods

In many respects the selection of security safeguards is an art based upon experience. Consequently, experienced personnel must be involved in the process of selection. They must

(1) be able to take a holistic view of an application — a systems approach (Checkland, 1981) is considered again in chapter 8
(2) have knowledge of common security methods
(3) be familiar with the information system under consideration and its vulnerabilities.

An organisation's personnel will have the expertise to fulfil (3) above. Checklists (Waring, 1978; FIPS 73, 1980) contribute to (1) and (2) above. Other methods that can help with (1) and (2) above are discussed in the following sections, including a methodology for the orderly selection of security safeguards. An outline of the methodology, which is based upon guidelines of the Bureau of Standards (FIPS 73, 1980), is shown in table 6.2. It is applicable to new applications and to amendments to existing systems.

No reference has been made to the operating system with which the new application software will interact because the boundary between operating system and application software varies considerably with different operating systems. Nevertheless, it is assumed that in most situations the operating system provides adequate security facilities, like monitoring and logging, to produce a computer environment in which the information system designer can proceed with confidence. It is the responsibility of the designer to ensure that the combined effect of all controls is satisfactory.

Table 6.2   An outline of a methodology for incorporating security features at the interface of and within application software

Phase of project	*Steps in design of security features*
(1) Feasibility study and analysis	1.1 Analysis of *vulnerabilities* of the application and its data
	1.2 Specify *security requirements* as an integral component of specification of user requirements
(2) Detailed system software	2.1 Design *interfaces* to eliminate specific risks
	2.2 Design sufficient *basic controls* to control and manage risks that cannot be eliminated
	2.3 Conclude design phase with a structured *walkthrough* of security safeguards
(3) Building the software	3.1 Control programming to eliminate effects of *errors* and deliberate *traps*
	3.2 Test how the system will respond to *unusual* and *fraudulent* inputs and how it will behave under unusual circumstances
(4) Post implementation	4.1 Check that planned security features within the clerical procedures and other manual activities are followed
	4.2 Incorporate additional necessary features into the contingency plan

6.3.1 A methodology for design of security measures in application software

A methodology is outlined in table 6.2 in which some of the suggestions shown can be seen to be normal design procedures followed by analysts. Therefore, reference will be made only to those aspects that have particular bearing on security. Many problems with software can be traced back to the feasibility study in which there is inadequate definition of security aims. The decisions about security requirements should be specified by users as general objectives, leaving designers to choose the most appropriate technical ways of meeting these objectives. It is often possible to achieve a certain security control either by administrative procedures or by controls in the software. It is preferable to use automated controls because they are less costly to operate and will be more consistently applied than manual controls. During the early parts of a development, it is necessary to identify threats and vulnerabilities. These will vary with each particular system and typical examples are shown in table 6.3.

Table 6.3   Threats, vulnerabilities and controls

Threats	*Vulnerabilities*	*Basic controls*
1 **Deliberate acts**	1 Poor development methods	1 Defensive design (that is, systems operate in a hostile environment)
1.1 Unauthorised input transactions	2 Access by many users	
1.2 Program modifications	3 Poorly trained data entry personnel	2 Auditability controls
		3 Encryption
1.3 File changes	4 Poor controls over preparation of source data	4 Individual accountability for interface
2 **Accidental acts**		
2.1 Input errors	5 Poor control over submission and distribution of data	5 Responsibility for sensitive objects
2.2 Processing errors		
2.3 Erroneous output	6 Professional computer staff do not regard controls over data entry as a professional challenge	
2.4 Curiosity browsing		

In the detailed design phase, the analysis must define the responsibilities of all individuals who interact with the application software through the interfaces. Each job function that connects to the application is an interface. Examples of interfaces are the points of (a) collection of source data, (b) data entry, (c) distribution of output, (d) computer operations, (e) audit, (f) program maintenance and (g) database maintenance. At each interface, the likelihood and consequences of accidental errors and of deliberate abuse of the interface are considered. This leads to identification of controls. It must be realised that although much of this analysis is directed towards the non-computer personnel, it is essential that similar analysis be brought to bear on the behaviour of computer staff. For example, some software utilities are so powerful that analysts and programmers should be allowed to use them only when under extremely strict management supervision, because with such utilities it is possible to change the internal features of a system during live operation and to do so without other parties being aware of the changes (Samocuik, 1982). This is a vulnerability and gives great scope for clandestine activity — the threat. Controls for this type of threat and others are available in the checklists referred to above.

At the end of the detailed design stage, there is advantage in having a structured walkthrough in which the security design is reviewed by a peer group consisting of user and computer specialists. A peer review is extremely effective because it allows the designer to receive formal professional advice from colleagues for a very small investment of time (Page-Jones, 1980). Structured walkthroughs can be used to advantage throughout the system development, for example to control programming and testing. Programming errors are a frequent cause of loss and once inserted into the code, irrespective of whether they are accidental errors or deliberate traps, are extremely difficult to detect. To prevent their occurrence, the best software engineering techniques must be applied, including static and dynamic testing. Dynamic testing uses test data to compare test results with expected results, but can test only selected parts of programs. Therefore, program analysers are used to assist with the testing process. An analyser collects details about another program during its execution. It can determine

- whether the test data has caused all statements of the program to be executed
- the degree to which the program has been exercised
- unusual, unexercised code which may be an unauthorised insertion.

Testing should ensure that desired functionality is achieved and that the application software will perform adequately under irregular circumstances.

6.4 Controls within application software and at the interface of the software

It is not uncommon for users of computers to complain that information is nonsense. The failure, seldom machine malfunction, is normally caused by human error. The clerical procedures, which are part of a computer based information system and which interface with the application software, are usually considerably more error prone than the application software. This section is concerned with basic controls which may be imposed in and around application software to reduce errors and achieve other security objectives. The places at which control can be exercised are shown in figure 6.2 and typical controls which can be built in and

Table 6.4   Typical safeguards that can be incorporated in an information system

Process	Typical safeguards considered during system design
1 Create source data	1.1 Source document design 1.2 Source document storage 1.3 Authorisation of source data
2 Prepare data for input	2.1 Batch documents close to point of origin 2.2 Batch size and serial number 2.3 Control logs showing details of transfer of documents
3 Input of data (includes conversion, editing and validation)	3.1 Convert data close to source 3.2 Restrict access to terminals and log unsuccessful attempts at terminals to gain entry to system 3.3 Validate data and batches
4 Processing	4.1 Control totals 4.2 Anticipation controls 4.3 Control logs
5 Output of data	5.1 Computer logs 5.2 Reconciliation procedures (for example, number of documents processed with those on batch controls)
6 Distribution of output	6.1 Control logs of dates and time of distribution 6.2 Reconciliation procedures for users (for example, expected output is received, cross-checks to ensure integrity) 6.3 Special procedures for highly sensitive documents
7 Data storage	7.1 File restoration procedures
8 Error handling	8.1 Procedures and reports to facilitate correction of errors and resubmission of data

around the software are shown in table 6.4. A more detailed discussion of this topic may be found in FIPS 73 (1980) and Squires (1980).

6.4.1 Source data control

A major operational objective is that data are recorded correctly and at the appropriate time. Data may be created in a machine readable form or in traditional handwritten form which is not machine readable. Handwritten source documents generally require and receive more comprehensive protection. Therefore the discussion below concentrates on handwritten documents because protection for these should be adequate for the special and more secure case of machine readable form.

In all cases control must be exercised over

- media — blank input documents must be safely stored and access restricted to authorised personnel
- design of format — good design of documents will encourage proper authorisation, provide an audit trail and ensure that data are accurate and complete; in many circumstances a sequence number on documents provides a basis for personal accountability
- special documents — special facilities require special protection; a form for adjustment of stock levels will be held by the auditor or senior personnel.

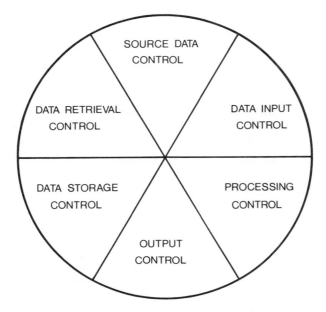

Figure 6.2 Data control in application software

In addition, authorisation procedures must be established. Authorisation will be proven by signatures on documents or passwords and identification codes (as discussed in chapter 3) for terminals. At each centre where source data are created, personnel will be selected by management to give authorisation to data that meet certain criteria; data not meeting the criteria are passed to a higher authority.

After source data are created, there is need to prepare for data entry which takes the form of manual checks by users. This additional work includes checking that documents have appropriate identification (for example, in the form of transaction number) to provide an audit trail, as follows

- batching documents in sets to enable reconciliation to be carried out at a later stage
- giving numbers to batches for accountability and for logging purposes
- maintaining control logs for batches of documents as they pass between different recording or authorisation points.

After source data has been processed, they must be systematically retained for a suitable period and later destroyed. Retention requirements vary with the information system which can be subject to legal constraints in addition to company backup and recovery plans. Similarly document destruction is influenced by the sensitivity of data involved but requires authorisation, supervision and logging procedures.

6.4.2 Data input control – verification and validation

Data verification is the procedure for achieving correct and complete transcription of data to machine readable form. Errors that are not detected during transcription may cause loss of data integrity and influence adversely management decisions. Data validation is the process of examining data to determine their accuracy, completeness, consistency and reasonableness. Invalid data can result in erroneous outputs and destroy the credibility of the information system.

The techniques that support data verification are as follows.

- Control totals: batches of transactions are grouped and important items are totalled. A total forms an additional input which stays with the batch and can be used for comparison purposes.
- Check digits.
- Visual verification: the keyed version is compared with the source data; this method is error prone and time consuming – it is advocated only for special situations such as direct data entry and must be supported by other controls.
- Key verification: source data are entered twice and the first and second sets of data are compared; any errors are rekeyed and reverified.

Data validation techniques that can be used to examine data to identify possible errors include control totals (for example, batch totals, record counts, and transaction balances) and checks for consistency, reasonableness and completeness. Data validation is an important basic control but it cannot compensate for weak controls elsewhere. Data validation is necessary

- during data collection and data entry before the data are used within the application software
- continuously as new data are generated.

Terminal entry systems are speedy but require a high level of automated validation. Invalid data should be corrected quickly but the correction process is itself subject to errors. For example, rejected data can often be left for a long time before correction is made; therefore, to ensure that data are not forgotten it is best if all invalid data are stored on a suspense file within the application system and removed only as a result of positive instructions from the user.

6.4.3 Control during computer processing

There are a number of general principles that can be followed to ensure that data accuracy and completeness are maintained during computer processing. Errors may occur despite accuracy of input data and machine reliability. Although computers have a high level of reliability, it is wise to build into the application software some detection and control features. Vulnerabilities include errors in the software, physical deterioration of magnetic media and data errors resulting from assumptions regarding the way arithmetic functions are performed. Controls can be established to overcome these problems. For example, direct access files can be taken offline during periods of inactivity in order to balance files and important elements of files or a database can be maintained with a running total which can be checked periodically to see that the new balance equals the old balance plus the running total. Other control mechanisms are exception reporting in which a report is generated if a program control is bypassed and anticipation controls which are based upon expected sequence of inputs.

However, perhaps the most useful and general basic control that can be used during processing and at other times is logging or journalising, which is the recording of selected events. Theoretically, the journal should contain a 100 per cent record of data and use of resources but practically this is not possible and the journal contains selected items, dependent on the security objectives of each individual system. A journal's contents can be decided only after appropriate analysis to identify details of data to be recorded, data retention period, analyses required and reports to be produced. A journal might typically hold

(1) nature of event: such as input or output of data or system usage

(2) identification of subjects and objects involved: people identifications and devices used
(3) information relating to the event: date and time, success or failure and appropriate facts concerning records before and after the event.

It must be remembered that a journal produced by an application system will only log activities performed by the application. Therefore, control checks must be carefully made through all logs. Journalising must be used selectively for if it is used to excess, detection of security violations can decrease because of communication overload or a computer can become overloaded with journalising to the detriment of more useful business activities.

6.4.4 Control of data output

A user judges an information system by the quality of the output. Therefore, output from a computer should not be released to users before checks have been made to ensure that the output is complete and accurate. The checks are made by a data control section which monitors work before and after computer processing. Considerable use is made of logs, such as the comparison of the log concerning input batches with the computer output details of processed and rejected batches. When output has been approved, its distribution to authorised users must be completed without loss of data or without interference. The method of distribution should be formalised with users after discussions. The result is the identification of authorised recipients, agreed distribution routes and transportation methods. Data control follows these agreed procedures and maintains a log containing date and time of distribution and name of recipient.

On receipt of the output, the recipient makes similar but more detailed checks and keeps a log showing reports received together with notes of queries referred back to data control. The user will keep special records for high security documents such as cheques and confidential information. The user is responsible for cheques and therefore will know the number of blank cheques in use and the quantity used in each computer run.

6.4.5 Control of storage and retrieval of data

Data on storage media must not be disclosed to unauthorised parties or accidentally or deliberately modified or destroyed. Data are especially vulnerable because storage and retrieval involves considerable human activity, especially by computer operators. Therefore, controls are essential and are provided through

(1) file handling processes of the computer system
(2) manual procedures for files when offline.

These controls are at the interface of the application software. The file handling processes are part of the system software and are governed by the controls discussed in chapter 3, namely authorisation, inference and cryptography. If a secure information system is to be developed, the designer must appreciate the strengths and weaknesses of these mechanisms. Data media when offline must be located in an area with a suitable environment and to which physical access can be restricted. The only person with access rights to the area is the person with responsibility for the data media. This is the data librarian who knows of all movements of media from the storage area and maintains a log showing (1) data media withdrawn, (2) destination, (3) authorising signature and (4) expected return time.

The protection of data media against destruction demands the maintenance of backup copies at other locations. It is a management responsibility as to which data are sufficiently critical and sensitive to require backup but once the policy is established, the creation and storage of backup copies away from the computer centre must be handled as a regular routine task. The two topics, control of offline data media and maintenance of backup copies, are considered again in chapters 7 and 11.

Table 6.5 Basic principles of security that can be used in design

Principle	*Explanation*
Non-secret design	A new system is improved if its features are exposed to criticism by many personnel, both designers and users
Acceptability to users	Each interface between the application software and users must be simple and natural to the user. If it is not, it will be bypassed
Complete mediation	Every access to every object must be checked to see if adequate authority is possessed
Default to access denial	If access is in doubt, access is denied because denial is preferable to unauthorised access

6.5 Summary

An information system should be designed on the assumption that it will operate in a hostile environment where it will be subject to frequent threat. In the past this has not been the case and consequently there has been a tendency to neglect the full implications of security until a system has become operational. If a system is to be secure, the application software must conform with the principles in table 6.5 (Hoffman, 1977). This can be partly achieved through the methodology and controls outlined in this chapter, but acting alone they are not sufficient. They need to be complemented by many other ideas and methods. For example, the data security aspects of authorisation, inference and cryptography considered in chapter 3 have limitations and the designer must act with due regard to the limitations. Similarly, the sophisticated method of threat analysis, presented in chapter 8, is an invaluable aid to the designer and must be used to complement the methods outlined above. A broad or holistic approach to security will create a comprehensive and integrated control environment. Consequently with respect to application software it is essential to (1) consider the organisational factors that influence security, (2) have a general approach for security design and (3) incorporate time-honoured basic controls in and around the software. Since this is not easy, it is crucial that security features of application software evolve through a participatory process between designers and users of information systems.

Questions

6.1 Security requires a mix of (a) legal measures, (b) technological measures, (c) physical measures and (d) administrative measures. If the legal measures constitute 6 per cent of the overall controls, how significant are the other factors?

6.2 List and describe four different controls that can be built into programs.

6.3 Consider any information system with which you are familiar and describe

    (a)   its major control points

    (b)   input programmed control mechanisms which can be applied to data between receipt of machine readable data and creation of valid input transaction files for processing and

    (c)   programmed control mechanisms for the production of computer output.

Relate the controls given in your earlier answers to those of figure 6.2. For the parts of the figure for which you have no control mechanisms list and describe additional features.

6.4 Is documentation control important? Explain.

7 Security Aspects of the Operation of Computer Facilities

After the application software has been developed and has satisfied acceptance tests, it forms part of the information system and the system enters the operational stage. During the operational stage, security must not be allowed to deteriorate, otherwise the effort expended in building controls into the application software will have been wasted. The work of the operations section is of major importance and must be reliable. A number of procedures can be used to complement the controls that are in and around the application software (IBM, 1976). The operational aspects which affect security include company policies relating to access to computing facilities; commitment and involvement of operations personnel; recovery planning; and maintenance of software and hardware. There are many other aspects of security that are conducive to secure operations. These include data security, physical security and contingency planning. These are described in other chapters, with which there is some inevitable overlap. The topics in this chapter are presented from the operations point of view.

7.1 Operational security and the use of logs

Operational security is concerned basically with company policies and procedures for the security of company data and computer facilities. Although some of these policies and procedures may be based upon external requirements, such as privacy legislation, the majority are formulated internally by management and are of two types.

(1) Safeguards, many of which have been considered in earlier chapters, specified during the development stage and built around and in the application software.
(2) Measures relating to the organisation and execution of operations activities.

There are a number of methods relating to this second type, including those such as control of data during input preparation considered in chapter 6; personnel practices considered in chapter 5; and responding to security variances (FIPS 73, 1980) considered in chapters 5 and 8. Journalising or logging is another method and this is referred to in chapter 6.

7.1.1 Operating journals

Operating journals give summarised details of programs run, files used, messages between the programs and the computer operator via the console and failures. Although computer printed journals are not easy to examine, it is essential that all operating journals are

- scrutinised
- stored for future needs such as audit.

Certain events are of special importance to managers and if possible they should be recorded in separate journals. Events that require special attention are

- equipment failures
- computer run restarts from checkpoints (a topic discussed later in section 7.5)
- failures of programs during operation
- file recoveries
- re-creation of files.

7.2 Approaches to the operation of computer facilities

Unauthorised use of computer resources is prevented by an amalgam of controls and restrictions imposed by management. One of the most important decisions relates to the number of people who should have access to the facilities. Access is controlled by the operating environment, of which there are three major types.

(1) Closed operations: the only staff who are allowed access to the computer are the operators who take requests and then oversee the processing.
(2) Open operations: any member of the staff may have access to the computer to complete processing required.
(3) Unlimited access through communication lines: the user has no need to visit the computer centre or to contact the computer operators.

There are numerous variations on these operating environments (Hsiao *et al.*, 1979) but the type of environment used by an organisation must be consistent with organisational objectives. A closed environment is suitable for a high-security military installation. It demonstrates that security mechanisms can cause inconvenience for users. In general, an operating environment must be convenient for the user, especially as many modern applications depend on online computer access, that is an unlimited access environment. This too has weaknesses. Although it is ideal for the user, it is very exposed to unauthorised actions by legitimate users. An environment must be such that it deters potential offenders and prevents or detects offences.

7.3 Operations staff

A well-designed system will run on the computer with little or no action from operators. However, the actions that the operator does have to take should be relatively straightforward and reveal virtually no information about the system or about the data being processed. In the case of direct data entry or remote job entry from terminals, the operator sees nothing concerning the input except the messages on the console. If work is submitted through a data control section, the system should operate in a similar way; the computer should control operations, giving only the minimum of information to operators. Details of any abnormal conditions or terminations that occur during processing should be reported only on the user's output. The output should be handled by few people since there should be no reason for computer operators to peruse output. It should be passed soon after processing to the data control department for sorting and post-processing. Output should be clearly marked by the computer to aid sorting and to minimise the danger of it going to the wrong user by accident. Work that is processed through the data control department is more vulnerable than work that is entered remotely from terminals because it is handled by many different departments and the rigorous access controls used with terminal users for identification and authorisation are not operable. Nevertheless with minimum staff interaction among operators, users, data controllers and file librarians, a secure operations environment can be created.

7.3.1 Training of computer operators

Computer operators, like other employees, cannot be expected to behave in the way outlined above and to act responsibly in security matters unless they are encouraged and trained to do so. Operators require general knowledge of the computer, the operating system, system control, safety and security of equipment and documentation. They need special training concerning routine operational duties, security tasks and security awareness. Security task training should make operators aware of things that they must not do as well as of tasks that they must do. Operators must know of positive actions to take in the event of fire and how to deal with intruders — people may stray unintentionally into prohibited areas and the operator must know whether to expel the intruder or to press the alarm button in order to obtain assistance. Security training appears to deal with the obvious but organisations that have initiated training plans have had favourable reactions, because it improves morale and makes the operators aware of the importance of their work.

7.4 Library management system

The continuity and effectiveness of computer operations are dependent on a library management system that uses good control procedures and standards to ensure the safe keeping and integrity of an installation's program libraries and data files. A secure library system is developed after consideration of the following factors

- media storage and protection
- access to media
- migration of programs from a test environment to a production environment
- emergency changes
- management policy and reporting needs.

The methods of media storage and protection are based upon identification of media that should be protected and recognition of personnel who have privilege of access to protected media. There should be clear differentiation between test environment where a program is created and production environment where a program processes live data. Security requirements dictate that before a program can be migrated to the production environment, testing must have shown that it conforms to design requirements and does nothing extra; once in the production environment the library system must protect the program from unauthorised amendment. The library system operates within a management policy which indicates steps to be taken in the event of unauthorised access to the library or the media. Management should receive regular reports showing activity of the library system together with details of unauthorised accesses and emergency changes of programs. Emergency changes are caused by incidents such as a program error discovered during a production run. Time constraints make it impossible for emergency changes to go through normal procedures of authorisation of change, testing and transfer to production environment. An emergency change creates a vulnerability. Therefore, each emergency change must subsequently have special attention to ensure that the library system is not compromised. Management must maintain close interest in emergency changes not only because of the vulnerability but also because a high percentage of such changes is indicative of other basic failures such as poor testing procedures. Further information on library management systems is in Gilhooley (1980). The library system must also be designed to counter a complete or partial loss of the libraries of programs and data files through countermeasures of recovery and backup procedures.

7.5 Short term recovery

There are people who believe that it is possible to build a computer based information system in which the application software is so reliable that recovery procedures are virtually unnecessary. This viewpoint, even allowing for the best software and most reliable hardware , is optimism bordering on imbecility. A better design approach is a cautious one in which the information system is believed to operate in a hostile environment. The advantage is that this encourages the designer to imagine the greatest range of misadventures that could occur; the misadventures help in the selection of security safeguards — this approach is risk management which is considered in detail in chapter 8.

Computer installations deal with minor failures virtually every day — for example, when an interrupted job is restarted — and the situation is retrieved in minutes or perhaps hours. This type of incident causes the delay of data processing or puts computing services temporarily out of action. It is illustrated in table 7.1 and requires a short term recovery plan. This contrasts with the incidents illustrated in table 7.2. These are disasters that destroy major facilities and require long term recovery — long term recovery planning or disaster planning are considered in chapters 8 and 11. Vulnerabilities that accentuate the requirement for short and long term recovery plans are shown in table 7.3.

In response to failure of information system components, the system must have recovery procedures which ensure that the computer based subsystem

- has minimum mean recovery time
- fails soft and continues to operate but with a reduction in level of service — this is referred to as graceful degradation (Watson, 1984)
- fails safe without being a threat to security
- is able to recover from any eventuality.

Table 7.1   Threats that delay processing and require a short term recovery plan

---

(1) Hardware failure, such as disk unit or major storage device
(2) Computer operator error
(3) Application software error
(4) Minor fire, such as disruption of media library, not total destruction

---

Table 7.2   Threats that may destroy a major facility and require a long term recovery plan

---

(1) Fire
(2) Natural disaster, such as flood
(3) Terrorist act
(4) Major industrial action

Table 7.3   Vulnerabilities that accentuate the need for recovery planning

---

(1) Business dependence on information system and computer processing, for example, organisation with no manual backup such as a bank
(2) Timeliness of processing is critical, such as for a hotel reservation system
(3) Centralisation of computing facilities

A number of mechanisms and strategies are possible for short term recovery, such as file backup, checkpoint restart and file restoration facilities.

7.5.1 Restart capability

Data processing can fail during a program run because of operation system failure, application program failure or file error. Experience has demonstrated that for failure of programs running for approximately 30 minutes or more, a restart facility is necessary whereby processing can start from a checkpoint within the program run rather than reprocessing from the start. For small systems a checkpoint might be taken at completion of each main file update and file restoration facility achieved by copying the file after the update.

In the case of a very large system involving the processing of many large files virtually without stops, such as with customer accounts and services in a large gas or electricity corporation, special facilities are necessary for recovery. The first is to take a copy of the state of the program at regular intervals — that is, take a check point which is a snapshot of the entire processing including memory and peripheral data. This information is stored on file and can be retrieved so that it is possible to re-create the program to its exact state at the instant when the check point was made. It does not restore the files to their checkpoint state and therefore the second special facility is one to restore files. The procedure is to store all record changes made since the last file copy; then the changes can be used with a utility to restore the file to be compatible with the checkpoint. There are two ways of achieving this.

(1) Afterlooks: copies of the records are taken after updating so that an earlier copy of the file can be rolled forward to the checkpoint by applying the afterlook records.
(2) Beforelooks: copies of records are taken before updating so that a later copy of the file can be rolled back to synchronise with the checkpoint.

The checkpoint feature and file restoration facility are part of the system software and are linked together so that all files in a system can be accurately synchronised.

7.6 Maintenance of software and hardware

Modifications to software and maintenance of hardware are essential for the evolution of any system. Unfortunately both cause threats. During program modification, errors can enter a program, which affect data integrity, or code can be deliberately inserted for dishonest activity. Similarly, while hardware is being maintained sensitive data can be divulged to maintenance staff.

Programming modifications should be subject to the same controls as normal programming (Waring, 1978) but a period of program modification is a transient state and therefore needs special attention, as explained in section 8.5. Additional protection that can be considered for software modifications includes regular and conscientious management scrutiny of all modifications; a comprehensive log of all modifications; and precise standards and procedures for authorisation, coding and testing.

Regular preventive maintenance is a necessity and if breakdowns occur often, as indicated by the hardware journals, then the frequency of maintenance must be reviewed. During maintenance all production data should be offline and the main memory should have all traces of data and applications software removed from it.

7.7 Summary

The work of computer operations is critical and it has been shown how this work can be made more secure. A potential offender needs access to and knowledge of the information system and its operation. Therefore, secure operating procedures depend on the enforcement of time-honoured practices such as separation of duties and the need to know principle. It is also important that security procedures built into the system are followed and not ignored. The onus lies with management. If management does not emphasise to personnel the need for security during routine operation of a system, then all the effort and planning in the design of security aspects will have been wasted.

Questions

7.1 Explain how batch control can be used in an online system. What are the disadvantages and what other procedures can be used to achieve similar control in an online application?

7.2 A log which records details of all transactions made by users on a database increases system overhead. Are there any other disadvantages?

7.3 Explain the meaning of *threat monitoring.*

8 Developing and Reviewing a Security Programme of an Organisation

In this chapter risk assessment techniques are discussed. These methods are used to identify the need for safeguards. Quantitative methods of risk assessment are explained and their difficulties of application are considered. A number of qualitative methods are also discussed.

A methodology for evaluation or development of a security programme is outlined. It addresses the question of security from a systems epistemology in the sense that the system whose security is under examination exists within a wider system. The methodology uses qualitative and quantitative techniques.

Unfortunately, safeguards cannot be guaranteed to protect in all circumstances and therefore there is need for contingency plans

It is essential to remember the importance of people in and around the techniques described. For example, the professional judgement of personnel is the basis of identification and selection of security safeguards and virtually all operational security devices are dependent to some degree on the competence of humans. People are fundamental components of security systems. Unfortunately they are often the weakest component.

8.1 Risk management

Developing a security programme for an organisation is achieved through three basic objectives, namely (1) risk identification, (2) risk analysis and (3) risk control. The three objectives are collectively referred to as 'risk management'. Risk identification involves a broad examination of a business to build up a clear picture of the potential risks threatening the organisation. Risk analysis, sometimes referred to as 'risk assessment' or 'evaluation', refers to a critical consideration of each potential risk to determine its likelihood of occurrence and the size of the loss if a potential danger area were to become an actual exposure. The third objective of risk management is to control risk and this necessitates decision taking based upon information obtained from risk analysis. The factors emanating from risk analysis (that is, potential impact or loss and likelihood of future occurrence) are weighed against each other in order to select the most appropriate course of action to take against each risk. The final outcome may be controls in the form of new procedures, new equipment or additional personnel.

In a situation where the aim is to review an organisation's security programme, it may be assumed that the organisation has already completed the three stages of risk management. Therefore, the objective of a review is to measure the adequacy of an earlier analysis.

An outline of a common procedure for developing and implementing a security policy for an organisation is

(1) analyse risks in order to provide a basis for developing a security policy
(2) select cost effective security safeguards to reduce exposure to losses
(3) implement appropriate security safeguards
(4) develop contingency plans for (a) backup operation, (b) disaster recovery and (c) emergencies
(5) train personnel
(6) plan and conduct security audits
(7) adjust security safeguards and contingency plans.

The procedure, outlined in figure 8.1, provides a means of identifying and distributing appropriate defence mechanisms. Success or failure of a safeguard is generally dependent on the attitude of people. Therefore, responsibility for each

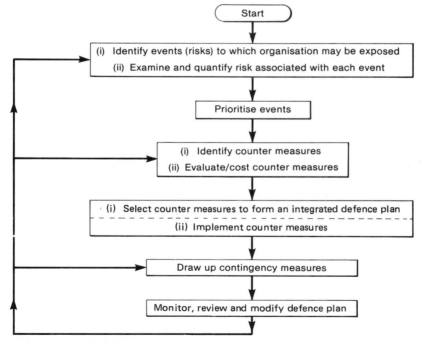

Figure 8.1   Risk management – developing a security programme for an organisation

Table 8.1   Responsibility for security

Organisational level	Responsibility for	Examples of detail
Top management	Organisational control environment	Initiate and approve contingency plan Act on all incidents of known violation of management security policy (such as illegal and unethical transaction)
User management	Data integrity	Establish procedures (for example, segregation of duties or authorisation procedures) Strive to employ, train and develop competent and trustworthy personnel with clear lines of authority and responsibility
	Confidentiality and data integrity	Establish physical and access controls to assets and data Establish and maintain check points and balances Monitor compliance with controls through scheduled and unscheduled audits
Data processing manager	Confidentiality, integrity and computer services	Ensure that hardware, software and computer operations meet security requirements
Personnel departments	Organisational control environment	Establish terms of employment and screening procedures consistent with company and department security aims

security measure is given to one department or unit of an organisation, as illustrated in table 8.1. The total security programme for all the information systems is the responsibility of many organisational units (FIPS 31, 1974).

8.2 Risk identification − a responsibility of management

Every organisation has a security strategy. The strategy may be one that has grown by accident or in response to difficulties that have occurred. The security posture that evolves in these circumstances may be perfectly satisfactory but is more likely to be one that is extremely vulnerable. The ideal development procedure is one in which the security programme is planned, directed and nurtured by the organisation's management. Even if the latter is the case, it is still not an easy task to develop a sound security programme because management is faced with the difficulty of selecting appropriate security measures that are cost effective. On the one hand security measures that are too elaborate can be an administrative and financial encumbrance. On the other hand a lack of appropriate safeguards can be equally or more costly if an attempted security attack, such as fraud, is successful. Therefore management must know (1) what is at risk, (2) the cost (that is, the loss) incurred if a risk becomes a security breach, (3) safeguards that can be implemented to reduce risk, (4) the costs of the safeguards and (5) the risk reduction that follows from the implementation of specific safeguards. At the centre of this type of approach is risk analysis (Courtney, 1977; Glaseman *et al*. 1977; Reed, 1977) which attempts to quantify the risk associated with each specific loss event. The overall objective is to provide management with sufficient information to make decisions for financial investments in security safeguards.

To obtain this management information, a risk analysis is performed with the objective of preparing a quantitative statement of the potential problems or threats to which an organisation's information systems are exposed.

8.3 Risk analysis

A procedure for risk management, which encompasses and uses risk analysis, is illustrated in figure 8.1. It is concerned with (1) identification, examination and evaluation of risks within an organisation and (2) use of countermeasures to attempt to contain losses to an acceptable minimum level. There are four approaches to handling risks, as follows.

(1) To avoid a risk: a system is modified so that a particular system feature and its associated risk are removed.
(2) To reduce a risk: security measures are used to reduce a risk to an acceptable level.
(3) To retain a risk: nothing is done about a risk, perhaps because it is small and insignificant.
(4) To transfer a risk: a system is left unchanged but the risk of loss resulting from a particular event is transferred to another organisation, for example by means of an insurance policy or a contract.

One mathematically based approach to risk analysis uses statistical data to analyse the risks in a given situation (Wong, 1977). Unfortunately there is seldom sufficient data for this method to be useful. In general, risk analysis is defined as any mechanism for providing information to enable management to make decisions concerning which risks or combination of risks are critical. Risk analysis is the basis of safeguard selection. It is a systematic approach for

(1) categorising threats to data
(2) categorising countermeasures to these threats
(3) deciding on a plan of action which will direct technical and non-technical resources to (a) the most likely risks and/or (b) the most expensive risks (Hoffman, 1977).

A number of methodologies for risk analysis have been proposed, including the Illinois approach of the economics of security (IBM, 1974), the Courtney approach (Courtney, 1977) and a method based on fuzzy set theory (Hoffman *et al.*, 1978).

In the Illinois approach, the total expected cost per annum to use the security system k is defined as

$$C(k) \quad + \quad L(k)$$

where $C(k)$ is the cost (in £/year) to install and operate the system k, and
$L(k)$ is the expected loss (in £/year) due to exposure, or the cost of exposure, when the security system k is in operation.

The total loss $L(k)$ is found by considering all possible threats, where threats are access routes to the protected assets, such that

$$L(k) = \Sigma\,[(\text{exposed value}) \times \text{probability of safeguard failure})]$$

The difficulties with this approach are concerned with making major assumptions in identifying and quantifying all possible access paths to assets and in estimating probabilities of failure of the protection mechanisms that block these paths. This type of approach encourages risk managers to attempt to make calculations more

Table 8.2   Parameters for cost of impact and frequency of occurrence

Estimated cost of impact	*i*	*Estimated frequency of occurrence*	*f*
£10	1	Once in 300 years	1
£100	2	Once in 30 years	2
£1,000	3	Once in 3 years	3
£10,000	4	Once in 100 days	4
£100,000	5	Once in 10 days	5
£1,000,000	6	Once per day	6
£10,000,000	7	Ten times per day	7
£100,000,000	8	A hundred times per day	8

precise than can be justified. For example, a long discussion as to whether an exposure will cause a loss of £73,000 or £83,900 is irrelevant because it makes little or no difference which value is chosen. Minor variations in the values selected may contribute significantly to the time required to carry out a risk assessment without any corresponding increase in the accuracy or the value of the analysis. Therefore, it is advantageous to analyse the risk in terms of order of magnitude, rather than actual magnitude; and to make correspondingly rough estimates of frequency of occurrence of loss. This is the approach advocated by Courtney who recommends an emphasis on relative magnitudes of impact and probabilities, as indicated in table 8.2.

8.4 Courtney risk analysis

There are two key elements in this risk assessment, namely a quantitative statement for each possible loss event of

(1) impact or cost if an exposure occurs, indicated by parameter i
(2) frequency of occurrence, indicated by parameter f (Lobel, 1980).

The ranges of the parameters, i and f, are shown in table 8.2. The parameters are used to calculate the annual loss expectancy L, where

$$L = 1/3 \times 10^{(i + f - 3)}$$

For example, if an event with a potential loss of £100,000 per occurrence is likely to happen once every three years then it is apparent that the annual loss expectancy is £33,333. If the above formula is used then table 8.2 gives $i = 5$ and $f = 3$, so that

$$L = 1/3 \times 10^{(5 + 3 - 3)} = 1/3 \times 10^5 = £33,333$$

Table 8.3   Annual loss expectancy

Value of i (related to cost or impact of event)	Value of f (related to frequency of occurrence)							
	1	2	3	4	5	6	7	8
1				£30	£0.3K	£3K	£30K	£0.3M
2				£0.3K	£3K	£30K	£0.3M	£3M
3			£0.3K	£3K	£30K	£0.3M	£3M	£30M
4		£0.3K	£3K	£30K	£0.3M	£3M		£300M
5	£0.3K	£3K	£30K	£0.3M	£3M			
6	£3K	£30K	£0.3M	£3M				
7	£30K	£0.3M	£3M					
8	£0.3M	£3M						

The values of *i* and *f* may be used with table 8.3 to find the loss. The table shows only rounded values for loss, which is consistent with using factors of 10 for orders of magnitude of impact and frequency of occurrence. To suggest that the loss is £33,333 implies a degree of accuracy that is not at all consistent with the lack of precision in selecting *i* and *f* values.

The calculation of the annual loss expectancy is at the centre of a broad methodology which in outline is as follows.

(1) Form a risk analysis team: a correct consideration of impact and probabilities can be achieved only if a multidisciplinary team is formed of competent senior representatives from data users and owners, the security department, the internal audit function and each section of the computer department (Reed, 1977).

(2) List the application systems on the worksheet shown in figure 8.2.

(3) List on the worksheet the data files used by each application.

(4) Assign values for impact and frequency of occurrence for each intersection in the matrix of the worksheet.

(5) Calculate the risk, *L*, on a cost per unit time basis for each pair of values in (4) above.

Name of system or data set		Accidental			Deliberate			Exposure (breach) if unable to process for:- hours					COMMENTS
		confidentiality / disclosure	data integrity / modification	destruction	confidentiality / disclosure	data integrity / modification	destruction	2	4	8	12	18	
	i												
	f												
	L												
	i												
	f												
	L												
	i												
	f												
	L												
	i												
	f												
	L												
	i												
	f												
	L												

Figure 8.2   A risk analysis worksheet

Table 8.4   Criteria for selection of a security safeguard

Security safeguard principle	Comment
(1) Cost effectiveness	Virtually all safeguards have a cost. The decision related to how much to spend on protection must take account of the value of the data and the professional responsibility of the data user to protect data
(2) Security not dependent on secrecy	It is assumed that an attacker will know of the presence of a protection device but that safety is still possible because of the invulnerability of the device
(3) Need to know or least privilege	Only the minimum amount of information is provided to a person or device. The amount is just sufficient for the person or device to carry out the functions effectively
(4) Independence of control from controlled	Personnel (such as auditors) should ensure that a security safeguard is independent of the personnel who are controlled by the safeguard
(5) Minimum human intervention	An ideal safeguard is one that needs no human intervention during its operation
(6) Failsafe default	When a fault occurs on a safeguard, the safeguard should failsafe
(7) Universal application	A security device should be applied uniformly over the entire device domain
(8) Completeness	Before coming into operation a safeguard must be proven

continued on page 120

Table 8.4 (continued)

Security safeguard principle	Comment
(9) Durability	A safeguard must function effectively over time (note that the performances of devices dependent on human intervention or support are likely to deteriorate with time)
(10) User acceptability	If a device places an unacceptable constraint upon a user, it is likely to be circumvented
(11) Monitoring	A safeguard should provide for monitoring of its proper performance, of its failures and of attacks to which it has been subjected
(12) Auditability	It should be possible to test a security device to establish if performance matches specification
(13) Accountability	One person should be held responsible for the operation of one safeguard
(14) Reaction to attack	A good safeguard will respond to attack with minimum damage to the asset that is under attack

Table 8.5   Illustrative examples of threats and safeguards

Threat	*Safeguard*
(1) Data security	
Threats to history-sensitive data	Inference prevention; logging details of queries
Threats to value-sensitive data	Access control and restrictions; partitioning; authorisation hierarchies
(2) Operating system security	
Flaws in operating system	Verification of operating system; kernel concept
Threats from unauthorised personnel	Logging; identification and authentication procedures; access control matrix
(3) Physical security	
Electronic and electromagnetic tampering	Cryptography
Intruders	Guards; passwords, locks, badges and keys.
Disasters	Site selection; backup plan; recovery plan

(6) Consider a safeguard and decide if it is cost effective using information from (5) above and if it is suitable on the basis of selection criteria shown in table 8.4 (Saltzer and Schroeder, 1975; Hoffman, 1977; Parker, 1981). Typical safeguards are given in table 8.5

Despite the fact that quantitative risk assessment using consensus techniques may provide useful information, it must not be forgotten that the resulting numbers are based upon a high degree of guesswork. Risk analysis remains essentially a matter of human judgement. As a consequence the Courtney risk methodology has been criticised because

(1) it is an expensive exercise, possibly not justifying its costs (Schweitzer, 1982)
(2) it is extremely difficult to select even rough values for the parameters i and f
(3) it is not a simple matter to understand and predict the kind of attacks that could be made on an information system
(4) the methodology does not provide a comprehensive basis for selecting risk reducing security measures and for estimating the corresponding effect on L, the annual loss expectancy (Glaseman *et al.*, 1977).

8.5 Heuristic methods as aids to risk analysis

The problems in developing a security programme for an organisation are considerable. Nevertheless, it is unusual to come across a specific situation of threats and impacts about which nothing is known. Although the situation may not be fully understood, there will be some fragments of information and people with hunches and rough rules of thumb. Strategies that use partial knowledge like this are referred to as 'heuristic' strategies. They are no guarantee of success but they are better than nothing.

A simple heuristic technique is a checklist. Often, this is a list that has been collected over a period of time by a number of practitioners and shows things and areas to consider. A high proportion of the risk analysis process can be achieved only through the use of heuristic techniques such as checklists. Checklists that will help in the development of a security programme are widely available (AFIPS, 1974; Waring, 1978; Davis and Perry, 1982).

Both risk analysis and the more general analysis in development of information systems make extensive use of herustic techniques. In addition to checklists, other possibilities (Martin, 1976) are (1) making use of previous situations to predict future security failures, (2) recognising that computer personnel are only human and therefore that (a) they are weaker at some things than others and (b) they create security vulnerabilities within their area of activities, and (3) recognising that failure is often associated with inadequate response to change.

The frailty and lack of proficiency of personnel highlight the need to give special attention to areas of design where designers are likely to show their imperfections. Therefore, basic assumptions about security and subsystem interfaces are fruitful areas to examine. The exposure analysis methodology (Parker and Madden, 1978; Parker, 1981) recognises the frailties of people and examines the exposure to loss on the basis of the number of people who can accidentally or deliberately cause loss.

This methodology can be used where the Courtney approach is not applicable. Personnel are categorised by occupation and skills and the methodology provides for inclusion of all personnel from the highest to the lowest, that is from chief executive to clerk. This method produces better results for threats from in-house personnel than for external threats and since most known losses are caused by people in positions of trust, it has obvious merit.

In order to overcome difficulties associated with responding to change, information systems are examined to identify all transient states and then security procedures are checked to see how they cater for each significant transient. Situations include time of personnel replacement, period of implementation of modifications to an application system and transitions from system operation to non-operation. Documented security breaches (Farquhar and Wong, 1983) demonstrate that the common time for setting fire to equipment is the early hours of the morning and that tape librarians damage files during the period of termination of employment. These examples clearly illustrate the relationship between change and failure.

The possibility of predicting future failures from previous ones is widely recognised. Often, personnel working in an organisation have a clear idea of local problems and risks. This knowledge may have been acquired as a result of earlier incidents, such as near-miss failures. Therefore, it is advantageous to collect this knowledge systematically by the use of a security problem reporting form. Unfortunately, it has been demonstrated that reporting forms, although good in theory, are not successful in practice because observers do not like submitting detailed reports. A more fruitful method is the critical incident technique (Spear, 1976) which requires no formal detailed report by the observer of the incident but for success it depends on the efforts of analysts who complete formal personnel interviews.

The use of previous incidents can be developed even further in scenario analysis (Parker, 1981). This approach can be used instead of the Courtney approach in situations where probabilities are unobtainable to a sufficient degree of reliability. Scenarios may be earlier real-life incidents or fictitious ones. Scenario analysis is extremely subjective. It parallels the Courtney approach but goes further in that it serves directly to evaluate and select security safeguards. The scenario analysis takes the following form

(1) for each threat, several scenarios are prepared which describe how the associated asset or assets might be exposed to cause a loss
(2) the scenarios are given to the relevant departmental managers
(3) the managers review the scenarios by rejecting some and revising others
(4) the scenarios are revised to form the input of step (1) above
(5) an iterative process of steps (1) to (4) is continued until a set of practical and plausible scenarios are collected which the managers believe represent the range of significant vulnerabilities together with (a) current protection, (b) proposed safeguard improvements and (c) deficiencies
(6) protection mechanisms are identified and selected and the scenarios, with the chosen safeguards added, are used again to authenticate the effectiveness of the safeguards. Scenario analysis has the advantage of being an excellent communication aid between the different disciplines involved in a security study.

8.6 Reviewing security in an organisation or initiating a security programme

It is common to use checklists as a basis for reviewing security. Although checklists are a very powerful aid, they carry the disadvantage of giving an illusion of thoroughness which can obscure real problems. A simple mechanistic review using checklists is insufficient because it can result in attention being directed on too narrow a set of vulnerabilities and so produces security safeguards that are operationally inadequate. A security programme depends on people and it is clear that the behaviour of people with their near-infinite complexities cannot be forecast with any great certainty. Therefore, when reviewing information systems security or initiating a security programme, it is imperative to use a combination of approaches

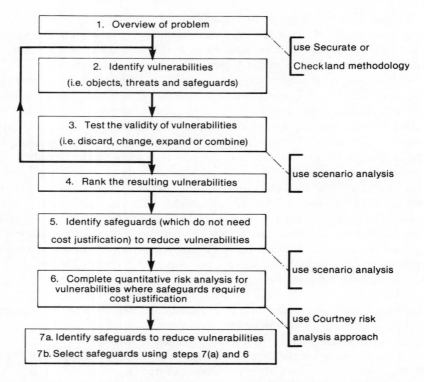

Figure 8.3   A methodology for initiation of security within an organisation

to achieve a holistic review which takes into account the fact that security is constantly changing because of personnel and technology developments.

A methodology for initiation of a security program is shown in figure 8.3. It is based upon an approach in (Parker, 1981). A review of security follows only the first three steps of the methodology but if security is inadequate the remaining steps are operated.

A holistic overview can be achieved through the Checkland methodology (Checkland, 1981) which is shown in outline in figure 8.4. In essence the objective of the methodology is to conceptualise a hypothetical perfect system and then to compare it with the actual (security) system to identify areas requiring improvement. It is illustrated in figure 8.5. The latter steps of the Checkland methodology would then combine with the first steps of the procedure of figure 8.3. In this way the Checkland methodology forms the framework within which to organise the study and encourages every important area to be explored. It is not a 'sausage machine' approach which when worked through gives the correct answer, but rather it helps to open up the situation by posing open-ended questions with many possible answers. This is important because good security requires a combination of technological, administrative and physical safeguards.

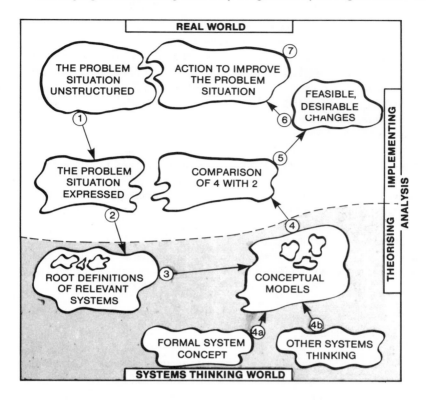

Figure 8.4 An outline of the Checkland methodology

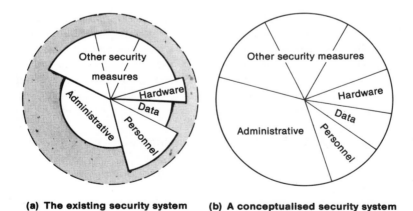

(a) The existing security system   **(b) A conceptualised security system**

Figure 8.5 Comparison of conceptualised security system and existing security system

Another way of achieving an overview is to use Securate (Hoffman, 1977) which is a computer based system for evaluation and analysis of a computer installation. It models the installation as a set of asset–threat–safeguard triples (A_i, T_j, S_k). Each asset (A) has a loss value, each threat (T) a probability and each safeguard (S) a resistance. The values are based on fuzzy set theory to provide security ratings for the installation and for subsections. With the help of a human decision maker, there is in Securate the potential to complete a security review, but experience has shown that it is most beneficial in 'increasing understanding of installation security' and it focuses 'thoughts into a well defined framework enabling the managers to view the situation more clearly and to gain insights' (Hoffman *et al.*, 1978).

The end-product of the overview will be the vulnerability triples (A_i, T_j, S_k). Several vulnerabilities may have the same asset or the same threat. The vulnerabilities are checked using scenario analysis and after modifications the resulting vulnerabilities are classified by size of risk. Safeguards are identified for those vulnerabilities that do not require cost justification. Quantitative risk analysis is made for the few remaining vulnerabilities in which possible safeguards may be difficult to justify because of lack of effectiveness and/or cost.

8.7 Contingency planning

Despite all the precautions of full and rigorous security procedures, it is impossible to eliminate risk and eventually something is bound to go wrong. Therefore the purpose of contingency planning is to ensure that swift action can be taken to achieve recovery with minimum loss if computing services are disrupted.

A contingency is an unscheduled interruption of computing services that requires measures outside of the day-to-day routine operating procedures. A contingency can vary from a trivial event, like a minor interruption of the electricity supply, to a disaster such as flood or fire. Other contingencies may result from explosion, failure of hardware, software faults, breakdown of air conditioning and industrial action of computing personnel. When an incident occurs the minimum of difficulty will be experienced if there are documented, realistic and reasoned procedures which have been rehearsed. Although it is impossible to make plans for all eventualities, the contingency plan must provide for

(1) standby procedures of operation for times during which normal services are disrupted
(2) recovery procedures after the cause of the disruption has been identified and corrected
(3) personnel responsibilities to achieve (1) and (2) above (Broadbent, 1979; Friedman, 1982).

The first and possibly the most important feature of a contingency plan is to define responsibilities in the event of an incident. Consequently, there is a coordinator or manager who takes control and decides what actions to take. Since actions include delegation of responsibility to members of an approved recovery team, the coordinator must have access to names, telephone numbers and addresses in order to contact the team members. The plan is not likely to be sufficiently detailed for many eventualities. Therefore, the coordinator must have confidence in the team in order for him to delegate quickly without going into detail.

Other features of a contingency plan are

- mutual backup arrangements with other installations
- lists of jobs that are important and jobs that can be suspended
- manual fall-back systems for operation during short duration stoppages
- membership of a disaster protection scheme. Organisations are often of the opinion that in the event of a major disaster computer hardware would be relatively easy to replace but that a computer room and its necessary support facilities would take considerably longer to obtain. Therefore they enter into a contract with a company that provides an empty room with ancillary services in time of need.

Irrespective of how well documented a contingency plan is, it is essential that parts of the plan are rehearsed before a real disaster occurs. This will ensure that it is practical and workable and that staff know what is expected of them. Organisations with well-conceived contingency plans have tested their plans by simply closing the door of their normal computer centre and instructing staff outside the centre to operate emergency services. Trials such as these usually highlight large gaps in the contingency plan. Problems occur because of simple things like inadequate supply of pre-printed forms or out-of-date user instructions and operations manuals. All aspects of a contingency plan must be reviewed and updated from time to time and in addition they must be rehearsed occasionally.

One essential updating requirement relates to new information systems. The contingency needs of each new application system should form part of the design process and therefore be part of the system specification and the clerical procedures manual.

8.8 Summary

It is important to recognise that in terms of developing a security programme no two computing environments are identical. Consequently each organisation and each information system within that organisation must be evaluated separately to determine the best protection strategy. It is difficult and costly to protect an existing information system that has been designed and implemented without regard for security implications. Security must receive full consideration during the design stage.

Within this chapter a number of techniques and methodologies have been presented for use in the development or review of security within an organisation.

The techniques can also be used within the design of an individual information system.

There are substantial difficulties in attempting a quantitative risk assessment. Not only is it difficult to put a precise monetary value to a threat but it is common for people to be unwilling to assign a monetary measure at all in situations where threats have a social impact, for example in the disclosure of confidential medical records. Estimating the frequency of occurrence is equally problematical. Natural events such as floods have been studied over a long period and consequently have associated with them a substantial body of useful data, whereas computer threats are relatively recent and too non-uniform to have allowed for the accumulation of practical statistical data. The application of numerical risk analysis is recommended for selective use after other qualitative methods have been used. In addition, in any business environment it is common, as indicated by the Pareto principle, for a few areas of risk to present the major proportion of the total potential risk. It is sensible to give these areas a comprehensive risk analysis examination.

The security development methodology outlined in this chapter uses a combination of qualitative and quantitative analysis methods. It provides the basis for a comprehensive appraisal of an installation which leads to an appropriate integration of technical, physical and administrative safeguards.

Despite all the safeguards, eventually something will go wrong. A contingency plan will minimise the loss. Contingencies may be small or large. Large contingencies may endanger the business itself. The capacity of a business to continue is a responsibility of the most senior executives of a company (Lane 1985). Therefore, contingency planning must be conceived across the whole organisation. Many organisations now depend to an increasing extent on computers for their continued operation but have minimal security precautions and contingency plans. If ill-fortune should occur, lack of prior analysis and preparation will bring serious criticism from those who put their trust in the executives.

Questions

8.1 A company is studying the risk to which it is exposed because of its dependence upon computers. It estimates a fire occurring once in 300 years might cause 100 per cent destruction of its total computing capability valued at £1 million; and a flood occurring once in 30 years might cause 10 per cent destruction. Calculate the annual loss expectancy from fire and flood using (a) your own method of calculation, and (b) the Courtney method.
Explain the difference in the two answers.

8.2 It is difficult to develop a security strategy for the information systems of an organisation. Is the development of a programme the responsibility of data processing management? Discuss.

8.3 Explain the meaning and usefulness of a heuristic method, a transient state and predicting future failures from past situations. Illustrate your answers with security examples.

8.4 The chief executive explained that the company had invested £80,000 in a security defence plan based upon a full risk analysis. He believed that 're-hearsals' were unnecessary because they disrupted routine daily operations. Discuss.

9 Privacy and Data Protection Legislation

Of the many threats posed by a breach of security of a computer based information system, perhaps the most controversial is that concerning the privacy of an individual or a group of individuals. However, this threat can be contained by technical, administrative and legal safeguards. In this chapter privacy concepts are reviewed as a basis for examining data protection legislation. In the developed world there is general recognition of the need for legislation but there is difference of opinion concerning the form that it should take. Clearly any legislation in this field affects systems analysis and design. Events in the United Kingdom during the 1970s are outlined because they enable the current legal position to be evaluated, and from there future legislative developments to be predicted. Although there is emphasis in this chapter upon events in the United Kingdom, the issues have universal relevance.

9.1 Privacy concepts and the impact of information technology

Although it is held sacrosanct by free societies throughout the world, privacy is not an easy concept to define, certainly not for simple legal enforcement. At the first international privacy conference in 1967 in Sweden, it was argued that privacy is a fundamental right and that all nations should prescribe civil and criminal legal safeguards to protect that right. Central to an understanding of privacy is the right to withhold specific aspects of our lives from other parties. However, modern societies have legitimate claims for information from citizens because it is virtually impossible to administer the infrastructure of government social services such as health and educational services without appropriate personal data. Furthermore, the administration of civil order and national security also necessitates access to personal data. Therefore, the nub of the problem is to provide for privacy of individuals or groups of people while allowing the state to carry on its legitimate tasks. While accepting that the freedom of the individual must be constrained in many ways in order to benefit the interests of the community, it is possible to formulate principles of good practice for processing of personal data (Ware, 1973; Linowes, 1977).

A typical set of principles is shown in table 9.1. They are the kind that are acceptable in general to governments of all free societies. Yet when the issue of privacy combines with computers massive controversy results. Why?

The data held in a manual system are exactly the same as in a computer based information system. The essential difference is the processing capability of computer based systems, as illustrated in table 9.2.

The difference is that computers make it possible for organisations to collect immense amounts of data about people. In a manual system it would be impossible

Table 9.1   Principles of good practice for the processing of personal data

(1) Openness	There must be no secret systems for personal data
(2) Access by data subject	An individual has the right to know what data are held and for what purpose they are used
(3) Limitations of use	An individual has the right to prevent data collected for one purpose being used for other purposes without his consent
(4) Participation of data subject	There must be procedures for an individual to correct or amend data concerning himself
(5) Accountability of data user	An organisation operating personal data systems is responsible for the reliability and use of the data

Table 9.2   Comparison of manual systems and computer based systems with respect to capability in processing personal data

Factor	*Manual systems*	*Computer based systems*
Effect of many large files	Slows down the process such that interrogation may be too slow and hence impractical	Little effect
Speed of response	Relatively slow	Quick
Ease of cross-referencing	Extremely difficult	Relatively simple
Ease of cross-referencing and linking various files	Extremely difficult	Relatively simple
Distance of interrogator	Distance reduces possibility of interrogation	Distance is insignificant

to manipulate such quantities of data. The inherent inefficiencies and natural constraints of manual systems are the protection of our privacy. Computers give data users the means of manipulating data. In addition, they may be integrated into national and international networks, so providing the capability to disseminate information over large geographically dispersed areas. The result of numerous public and private bodies collecting personal data on large groups of individuals using computers and communication networks is a substructure of information covering virtually every citizen. Not surprisingly there is anxiety about this and the main areas of concern can be categorised as

(1) size: large amounts of personal data are collected
(2) lack of integrity: there is evidence that inaccurate data are often processed
(3) insecurity: lack of adequate safeguards causes considerable risk
(4) lack of involvement of the data subject: the subject is the person whose personal data are being processed; often data are transferred from one application area to another or even from one business to another business without the consent or knowledge of the data subject.

If these four features are compared with the principles of good practice outlined in table 9.2, it is apparent that there is cause for alarm.

9.2 Privacy events during the 1970s in the United Kingdom

Consideration of events in the 1970s helps to evaluate current proposals of Government and to speculate on future legislative measures.

The possibility of and the need for privacy legislation have been discussed in Britain for nearly 20 years. This debate was echoed in other nations, especially in North America and Western Europe. However, as illustrated in table 9.3, a number of countries, unlike Britain, actually implemented data protection legislation in the 1970s. The fact is that by the beginning of the 1980s the United Kingdom was a member of a small minority group of advanced nations that had not enacted laws for the protection of personal data even though there had been considerable pressure on British governments throughout the 1970s to introduce legislation. This pressure came from sources such as

(1) individual Members of Parliament
(2) pressure groups, such as the National Council for Civil Liberties
(3) reports initiated by government (for example, the Younger Report and the Lindop Report)
(4) companies anxious that absence of adequate privacy legislation might put them at a trading disadvantage compared with companies in countries that have appropriate privacy legislation.

Table 9.3   Examples of personal data protection legislation in different countries

Nation	Legislation	Year
Sweden	Data Act	1973
USA	Privacy Act	1974
West Germany	Federal Data Act	1977
Canada	Human Rights Act	1977
France	Data Processing and Freedom Act	1978
Norway	Personal Data Registers Act	1978

9.2.1 The Younger Report

Between 1970 and 1972 the Younger Committee examined privacy. Its terms of reference were limited to privacy in general within the private sector only. The aspects of privacy investigated were

(1) unwanted publicity (by press and broadcasting)
(2) misuse of personal information
(3) intrusion in home life
(4) intrusion in business life
(5) modern technological developments (including surveillance devices and computers).

Only a small part of this investigation focused on the implications of computer based systems.

The Younger recommendations (Cmnd 5012, 1972) are outlined in table 9.4. The Report received a mixed response, particularly because of the somewhat optimistic proposal that data users adhere to its recommendations on a voluntary rather than on a compulsory basis. The Report suggested that the investigation

Table 9.4   Recommendations of the Younger Report related to computers

(1) Information should be held for a specific purpose
(2) Access should be confined to authorised users for the specific purpose for which the information was provided
(3) The amount of information collected should be a minimum consistent with the achievement of the specific purpose
(4) Information for statistical purposes should be held such as to remove identifiers from the rest of the data
(5) Data subjects should be notified about data held concerning them
(6) Maximum periods of retention should be specified
(7) There should be procedures for correction and updating of data
(8) Systems should be monitored for violations
(9) Care should be taken in coding value judgements

should be extended into the public sector but its main merit was that it prepared the way for the Lindop study.

9.2.2 The Lindop Report

In contrast with Younger, the Lindop study concentrated upon computer based information systems. In 1975 the British government announced its intention to prepare legislation for data protection and to create a statutory Data Protection Authority (Cmnd 6353, 1975). A committee under the chairmanship of Sir Norman Lindop was formed to advise the government on legislation. After initial work in defining the meaning of privacy, the Lindop Committee decided that the fundamental issue was data privacy where an individual lays claim to the control of circulation of information about himself or herself (Miller, 1971; Westin 1972).

Table 9.5   Outline of the Lindop Report for main components of a
             Data Protection Act

Data subjects
(1) Should know   (a) what information about them is held
                             (b) why it is held
                             (c) who will use it
(2) Should be able to check that
                             (a) the information is accurate
                             (b) only relevant data are used for a defined
                                  purpose

The Data Protection Authority (DPA)
(1) A DPA should be established to draft specific Codes of Practice for
     various groups of personal data processing applications
(2) The Codes should take the form of subsidiary legislation and acquire
     force of law

Breadth of application
(1) All personal data processing applications in the private sector and in
     central and local government should be called in by the DPA for
     registration
(2) All records, both 'hard' records (such as crime facts) and intelligence
     data, should be subject to the law unless the data have a direct bearing
     on national security
(3) A register of applications with basic details, including Code of Practice
     applicable, should be open to the public

Special cases
(1) At the discretion of the DPA, parts of the register may not be open
     to the public
(2) The Secretary of State should have power to give exemptions from the
     purview of the DPA. This should be limited to applications of national
     security

The final report has a separate chapter dealing with each of many areas of concern, including central government, the National Health Service, police and security services, education, employment and a unique personal identifier.

The study was completed in 1978 and some of its major proposals are shown in table 9.5. The report recognised the difficulty of maintaining a balance between the privacy of the individual and the legitimate claims of organisations. It was not sympathetic to the national use of a unique personal identifier but it attempted to create a framework that would not place any unreasonable or arduous constraints on data users (Cmnd 7341, 1978). It suggested the creation of a Data Protection Authority and took considerable care to define the composition and the role of this agency.

Again the Government response was not favourable. One objection was that the proposal for Codes of Practice would necessitate major extensions to criminal law, thus creating numerous new criminal offences.

9.2.3 Events between 1978 and 1984

Since the Lindop Report, successive governments — to the chagrin of many organisations (Simons, 1982) — have been reluctant to introduce legislation, fearing perhaps that effective data protection might be expensive to operate. In the meantime circumstances have changed. At the time of preparation of the Lindop Report, the computer market was dominated by mainframe computers used by large organisations. Since then the proliferation of minicomputers and microcomputers has effected massive changes. This has not made the implementation of data protection principles easier.

9.3 The international scene

At the time of publication of the Lindop Report, many nations had already passed data protection legislation, as indicated in table 9.3. More recently a Council of Europe Convention on Data Protection has been formulated with the purpose of securing respect for the rights and fundamental freedoms of individuals, not least the right to privacy. The Convention includes the following proposals.

Article 3   The Convention will apply to the public and private sector (a country can apply for exemptions).

Article 9   Exemptions will be granted only in the interests of public safety, state security, fiscal interest of the state or similar situations.

Article 12   Signatories will not impede the flow of data between itself and other signatories.

European nations are now under increasing pressure to ratify the Convention.

9.4 Areas of concern

In every country in which data protection has been under scrutiny, two major areas of debate have arisen. The first relates to the principles of good practice for processing of personal data. The second is the identification of organisations that cause concern. With respect to the latter, similar organisations are always identified and typically these include police, medical services, local and central government and the national security services.

A high proportion of data kept by organisations is not of a sensitive nature. However, data kept by the above organisations are often sensitive because unwarranted disclosure of certain types of information could affect an individual's reputation, employment or marriage. Clearly, when an individual provides data to an organisation, that person has an interest in the security of the data, in knowing to whom the data are available and whether they are being recorded correctly. If that same individual approaches an organisation for information about the data, it is not unusual for him or her to be told that the information is confidential; meaning paradoxically that virtually the only person who cannot see the data is the data subject who is most affected by the data (Rule, 1974).

The security services are always considered as areas of concern because of their very secretiveness. It is impossible to know of their activities especially as questions about their activities raised even in parliament are generally unanswered. Their success in maintaining secrecy is well illustrated by the fact that between 1978 and 1982 the installation of a computer with 20 gigabytes of online storage, capable of keeping data on millions of people remained secret (Simons, 1982). This venture, which was to create a massive secret computer system for MI5, the body concerned with internal national security, occurred ironically while the Lindop Report was being debated and the plans were unknown to Parliament. In situations that are intended to be secret, inaccurate or irrelevant data may cause irreparable damage to an innocent citizen (BBC, 1981).

Computer technology has proved of great assistance to the security services and the police. The police collect two types of data; hard facts and intelligence data (Cmnd 7341, 1978). Both types can threaten privacy but it is intelligence data, subjective by its very nature, that causes greater concern. Great danger exists if these two types of data are mixed indiscriminately (Bunyan, 1979). Special Branch is an arm of the police but there are no British laws to govern what political information Special Branch may secretly collect. Society gives unique and great privilege and power to the police. It is apparent from evidence worldwide, from nations of all political shades, that without safeguards this power will be misused.

The Lindop Report deals comprehensively with these and other areas of special concern.

9.5 Legislation

A data protection bill was placed before the United Kingdom Parliament in June 1983. It purports to fulfil two purposes

(1) to protect the data subject from threat of (a) correct use of incorrect information and (b) incorrect use of correct information
(2) to satisfy the requirements of the Council of Europe Convention on Data Protection to allow British industry to trade freely in Europe.

In the following year the Data Protection Act 1984 was enacted. This establishes a Data Protection Registrar who maintains a 'register' of data users and computer bureaux. Data subjects have legal rights including a right of access to their personal data. A Tribunal helps to resolve any differences between a data user and the Registrar. Data subjects who suffer damage as a result of inaccurate data or because data are not properly protected will be entitled to compensation from users.

9.5.1 The Data Protection Act 1984

Similar to legislation in general, the Data Protection Act is complex and to comprehend its implications it is necessary to consider it in the context of related features of other legislation. For example, it is not the first British statute to give to individuals the right to examine and challenge information that others hold concerning them – the Consumer Credit Act 1974 gives individuals these rights with respect to credit agencies.

The Act has forty-three sections grouped under five parts which are: I Preliminary; II Registration and supervision of data users and computer bureaux; III Rights of data subjects; IV Exemptions; and V General. In addition, there are four schedules which are explanatory and relate to the data protection principles, the Registrar and the Tribunal, appeal proceedings and powers of entry and inspection. The eight data protection principles of Schedule 1 are outlined in table 9.6.

For each registration, details as shown in table 9.7 are required (Court, 1984). If an application for registration is refused or if a deregistration notice is served on a data user, the user may appeal to the Tribunal. The Registrar has powers to ensure that personal data are used in accordance with the data protection principles. A person guilty of an offence under the Act is liable to a fine and data connected with the offence may be forfeited or destroyed. The only criminal offences under the Act are those connected with registration, for example failure to register or failing to comply with an enforcement notice. In other circumstances it is the data subject who must take civil action.

9.5.2 Exemptions

The Act applies only to personal data that are processed automatically. Consequently, data processed manually are totally excluded. In addition, specific types of computer applications are allowed exemptions from some or all of the requirements of the Act. These exemptions fall into two broad groups, namely

(1) applications which of themselves pose no threat to data subjects — for example, personal data held for domestic requirements
(2) applications which are critical to the interests of state or public agencies — for example, crime and tax data.

An exemption can be from

(1) subject access rights — as illustrated in table 9.8, access exemptions include data processed for crime detection, mental and physical health, taxation and social work.
(2) non-disclosure rules — in certain situations, as illustrated in table 9.9, data can be disclosed to a recipient who is not described in the data user's register entry.
(3) all parts of the act — as illustrated in table 9.10 data held for national security purposes are completely exempt from the Act.

Table 9.6   Data protection principles of Schedule 1 of the United Kingdom Data Protection Act 1984

Personal data held by data users
(1) Personal information shall be obtained and processed fairly and lawfully
(2) Data shall be held and used only for specified and lawful purposes
(3) Data shall not be disclosed or used in any manner incompatible with the purposes for which the data are stored
(4) The amount of data held for any purpose shall be adequate, relevant and not excessive related to that purpose
(5) Data shall be accurate and, where necessary, up to date
(6) Data shall not be kept for a period longer than is necessary for the purpose specified

Access rights of data subject
(7) A data subject shall be entitled to have
● access to personal data of which the individual is the subject
● access at reasonable intervals and without undue delay or expense
● data corrected or erased, where appropriate

Security measures
(8) Data users and computer bureaux are required to take appropriate safeguards to protect data from unauthorised access, disclosure, alteration or destruction or accidental loss

---

Table 9.7   Registration details

(1) Name and address of data user or computer bureau
(2) Description of data to be held and purpose for which the data are held
(3) Sources from which the data are to be collected
(4) Identification of persons to whom the data user intends to disclose data
(5) Name of foreign countries to which data will be transferred
(6) Name and address of person who will deal with requests for access from data subjects

Table 9.8   Circumstances in which a data subject is not entitled to access to data

(1) Data for law enforcement
Where data are held for law enforcement and revenue purposes and access to them may prejudice these purposes

(2) Data for financial services
Where data are held by certain bodies for regulating those providing financial services. (Note that these data are covered by the Consumer Credit Act 1974)

(3) Legal and judicial data
Data that are legally privileged and data concerning judicial appointments

(4) Statistical data or research data
Those data that are held for statistics and research purposes and are (a) never used or disclosed for other purposes and (b) never made available in a format from which individuals can be recognised

(5) Backup data
Data held to back up the data actually on the computer in case they are corrupted or destroyed

(6) Data for social work and physical or mental health
The Secretary of State may make an order exempting these data from subject access or making special arrangements for granting access to these data

Table 9.9   Circumstances in which data can be disclosed without the recipient appearing in the register entry

The disclosure relates to
1.   law enforcement
2.   revenue purposes
3.   national security
4.   legal proceedings
5.   prevention of injury or damage to health
6.   the data subject has consented to the disclosure.

Table 9.10   Total exemptions from the Data Protection Act 1984

The following categories are completely exempt but some of the exemptions are conditional and it is essential that one complies completely and absolutely with the conditions.

1. Data held for national security
2. Data held *only* for payroll or pensions
3. Data held *only* for accounting purposes
4. Data held *only* for preparing the text of documents
5. Data held *only* for domestic purposes
6. Data held for mailing lists

In table 9.10 there are exclusions which are of significance to the data processing industry, including data in mailing lists of names and addresses that are held with the approval of the data subject and comply with restrictions on disclosure. The conditions attached to each exemption are critical and none more so than those which are connected to data held

(1) only for payroll or pensions or
(2) only for accounting purposes and making financial and management forecasts.

If exemption is claimed by a data user, it is essential that the data user is aware of all the rules and is able to adhere to them completely at all times.

9.5.3 Implementation

The date for first registrations is September 1985. To help organisations with the implementation of the Act the Registrar is to provide a series of guidelines. In February 1985, the first guidelines were circulated to computer users. This publication advises users to

- appoint a data protection officer
- inform staff of changes to security
- complete a census of data used
- consider whether they qualify for exemptions.

It is advantageous for the data census to include classification under the following headings

- personal data held in manual systems
- personal data held on computer files
- non-personal data
- sensitivity levels.

Although the identification of personal data held in manual systems may be important initially with respect to exemptions, it may be more significant in the longer term because data that are now held on manual records may be converted to computer files in the future, especially with the proliferation of software products and microcomputers.

9.5.4 Costs and criticisms

During the passage of the Bill through its various stages, the financial effects of the legislation were discussed. Costs of the Registrar and his office plus the Tribunal were estimated at £0.65 million per year — monies that will be recovered from registration. The cost to government departments of developing hardware and software was estimated to be some £5.5 million over the first two years. However, it is extremely difficult to estimate the cost of providing access to data subjects; it was suggested that if access rates were 0.1 per cent the operating costs might be £1 million per annum. The implementation costs and operational costs for local authorities and public bodies were placed at £10 million per annum and £13 million per annum respectively. Private companies would incur the same type of costs — setup costs and recurring operating costs. Experience in other European countries is that the level of access by data subjects is very low and claims for compensation for damage caused by data inaccuracy are minimal.

It can be concluded (Wong, 1984) that the considerable costs that organisations incur far outweigh the benefits that accrue. A different view of the Act (Gostin, 1984) is that although it is welcome it 'will be ineffective in safeguarding personal records, inefficient in operation and will not meet the needs of our European trading partners.' These criticisms stem from a number of worries including:

- the failure to cover manual records
- the omission of the need for codes of practice so that detailed interpretation of the law is left to judges in civil courts,
- anxiety about the critical watchdog role of the Home Secretary which might conflict with his wider responsibilities to many government departments which hold extremely sensitive data.

9.6 Summary

Today citizens are counted, watched, recorded and questioned by more government and private organisations than at any time in history (Norback, 1981). As a result of this larger pool of personal information, combined with the greater details contained, there is greater risk than ever of personal confidential information falling into wrong hands. Therefore, data protection legislation must provide safeguards that respond to the needs of a citizen without disrupting the basic and essential flow of information to, from and within organisations.

In the United Kingdom there is broad concensus on the need for effective data protection legislation. Unfortunately, the issue has many complicating facets which have resulted in considerable but inconclusive debate about the form that legislation should take. The final outcome of these discussions will be influenced by technical, commercial and civil rights factors. The experience of other countries will also play a part. For example, in France it is reported that at the beginning of 1982 approximately only one-fifth of the 150,000 organisations in France that were eligible for registration had actually registered. Nevertheless, it is clear that pressures for legislation which have grown throughout the 1970s, will continue during the 1980s, even after initial legislation is completed (Hoffman, 1980).

Existing legislation varies considerably from one country to another. This is patently unsatisfactory because if data are transferred from a country with sound legislation to another with inadequate safeguards, then the data become insecure. While international pressures for common regulations grow, in Europe the situation remains mixed. Many countries have already enacted data protection legislation and this, combined with the Council of Europe Convention, will ensure that the problem in Europe is resolved fundamentally, if not completely, in the near future.

Privacy legislation affects the design and operation of information systems. While registration will be an integral part of development, the major consequence will be that system designers will be required to provide for an unprecedented level of security and end-users will look to designers for advice on how systems can be made to comply with the law. There will be a large number of existing and new systems to be approved. Overall there will be a significant cost increase. In the USA attempts have been made to estimate the financial impact of implementation of privacy controls (Goldstein, 1976). The implications of such legislation are not limited to the development but also impinge upon the operation of systems. Means of checking that information systems operate within the law must be devised. One way of achieving this is through a privacy audit (Deloitte *et al.*, 1982) which might be made at the same time as the financial audit. Nevertheless the argument that the high costs of data protection are an insurmountable problem is invalid because what is at stake is a fundamental issue of human rights directly concerning our quality of life.

Questions

9.1 "The inherent inefficiencies and natural constraints of manual systems are the protection of our privacy." Discuss.

9.2 It is not easy to design information systems to satisfy privacy legislation. Nevertheless explain the design features necessary to provide for

    (a) the right of an individual to know of data being kept concerning that person

   (b) the individual's right to inspect the record

   (c) the assurance of compliance with the regulation that data are only used for stated purposes.

9.3 A company wishing to comply with data protection legislation will incur (a) implementation or set up costs and (b) recurring operating costs. Explain the basic components of these costs.

9.4 European experience indicates that the level of data subject access has been low and damage compensation for data inaccuracy minimal. If this applies equally in the U.K., "the substantial costs which organisations must pay out to fully comply with the new Act would seem to be out of proportion to the benefits involved." (Wong) Discuss.

9.5 A company has an information system which contains personal data concerning people outside the company. The existing system is a manually based system. Discuss the factors that would influence the decision whether or not to change to a computer based system.

10 Protection of Proprietary Software

Piracy of micrcomputer software is a common crime. Protection of software has implications for owners, users and creators of software and for the general public. Protection can be achieved by legal methods and technical devices. Three areas of law, namely patent, copyright and trade secret, offer potential protection to programs. However, adequate protection can be achieved only through a combination of legal and technical deterrents.

10.1 The case for protection

Traditionally the computer industry has attempted to create software that is portable and easily usable. This implies use of standard versions of operating systems, compilers and interpreters. Piracy or illicit copying refers to the activity of obtaining another party's software, perhaps making minor changes to the coding, and then making financial gain by using or selling the software. Portable software makes piracy easy. The quest for portability of software is at variance with the need for protection.

Piracy of software for mainframe computers has never been a major problem. An important reason is that mainframe computer users with their large budgets have needed and been able to afford official software which provides training, updates and technical support. The support of the supplier is an integral and essential component of the software. The characteristics of the microcomputer market are different. The computer users are not supported by large budgets and are often parts of small businesses. In addition, the microcomputer is associated with the mass market. Consequently, microcomputer software has been afflicted by piracy. For example, the Wordstar package is reported to have three pirate copies in use for each genuine article. It is also reported that one-quarter of all microcomputer software suppliers suffer significant piracy.

Protection of software against piracy is of major interest to owners, users and creators of software and to the general public (Stern, 1982). This is illustrated in table 10.1 which shows that the interests of the parties vary widely and are in conflict. The conflict of interest, combined with the legal complexities, may explain why the problem of software piracy has not already been resolved.

Table 10.1 Groups with an interest in software protection

Group	Group objective	Objective calls for
Owners of software	Protection of financial investment	Maximum legal protection
Systems analyst and programmers	Greater recognition for creators of software (therefore protection desirable but computer personnel generally favour their relatively free access to new ideas)	More protection than at present
Users (for example, companies)	Software at minimum cost	No protection in short term (in the longer term, this would reduce amount of new software development and so would increase cost to user)
General public	Spread of knowledge and avoidance of wasteful duplication (balanced with adequate reward for real contribution)	Minimal protection

10.2 Methods for protection of proprietary software

In addition to technical safeguards, there are three areas of law, namely patent, copyright and trade secret, that offer potential protection to proprietary software (Mooers, 1975; Franz *et al.*, 1981; Graham, 1984). Each imposes restrictions on the author and presents problems related to definition of computer software.

The three legal areas as practised in the United Kingdom are considered, and experience in the USA is also discussed because of greater use of both computers and litigation there. The overview of the legal framework in the United Kingdom, shown in table 10.2, demonstrates how the structure and concepts of copyright, patent and trade secret law have evolved to provide adequately for specific non-computer situations. Consequently, they relate much less satisfactorily to software.

10.3 Copyright law

Historically it has been publishers and printers, rather than authors, who in the United Kingdom have sought protection for writings. Various legislation has been created over the last 200 years, culminating in the Copyright Act 1956. Part I

Table 10.2   Typical periods of protection and application areas of existing law

Law	Period of protection	Number of parties affected	Application areas
Copyright	Life of author plus 50 years	Infinite	Literary works
Patent	20 years	Infinite	Novel, inventive industrial application
Trade secret	Until the secret becomes public	A small number	(i) Ideas (ii) Even applicable to programs if beyond conceptual stage
Contract rights	For that period agreed by the parties	The signatories	(iii) Any methods that are known to only a small number of parties

of this Act refers to copyright protection of literary work (that is, to written or printed words) and it is under this part that software may receive protection. Part II refers to entrepreneurial rights in films and sound and other recordings. This Act has been criticised for failing to spell out basic principles in a manner of a true code (Cornish, 1981) and within the Act there is no reference to computers. In 1977, an official report suggested that there was urgent need to amend copyright law to provide for the advent of new technology (Cmnd 6732, 1977).

With respect to general literary works, copyright is allowable to any work that required skill, labour and judgement in its creation. In addition, the literary work must demonstrate originality. Originality means that the author must be the originator, not that the concepts contained therein are novel. This is a narrow definition but as a consequence of its narrowness there are advantages, including

(1) originality is not subjective but objective and therefore courts are able to decide relatively easily whether or not a work should be granted protection
(2) general protection is available to a wealth of literary works.

The position with respect to the application of copyright to software is not perfectly clear because of the low volume of litigation. However, at the present time several large videogame companies are arguing that other companies have infringed their copyright in videogame programs contained in erasable, programmable read-only memories, by copying and then selling copies. Many such cases are settled out of court and consequently it may be some time before a United Kingdom court decides whether or not programs are protected by copyright. It is possible that events may be overtaken by new legislation. Both the Banks Report and the Whitford Report gave support for programs to be given copyright. The Whitford Committee also helped to clarify the status of software by saying that "writing" could refer to other methods of recording information, including storage on disks or tapes. This has not been incorporated in legislation. Legislation, if not imminent, is anticipated because of a government Green Paper (Cmnd 8302, 1981). The Green Paper proposes that protection should be given to computer programs as literary works.

In the USA two different types of copyright can be claimed. They are

(1) at federal level, a work is copyright if it is published with the © mark and registered with the Copyright Office.
(2) at state level, a work is copyright under common law as soon as the work is produced, even if it is not published.

Programs have been eligible for copyright at a federal level since 1964 when the Copyright Office decided to accept programs as books with the proviso that the programs be in a form readable by humans. Between the years 1964 and 1978, only one-thousand programs were registered out of an estimated three million. No litigation arose.

In January, 1978, a new Copyright Act came into effect which gave developments in new technology explicit protection under statute, not common law. The Act gives the author the right to make translations into other languages and dialects. Recent conflicting decisions of federal tribunals illustrate that this new copyright law is not a problem-free method for the protection of object code in a read-only memory (ROM) nor for other forms of software (McLening, 1983). One case relates to a purpose-built ROM which formed an integral component of a chess game (Stern, 1982). The plaintiff alleged that the ROM had been stolen by the defendant by unloading the ROM and then transferring the unloaded code to a new master ROM for copying. The court said that there was no breach of copyright on the basis that buildings made from architectural plans are considered not to be copies. The legal analysis is that an architectural plan is copyright, but not the building; similarly the source program is protected as a writing, but the object program is in effect a mechanical tool like the building and thus incapable of protection under copyright law. In another case concerning a coin-operated video game, it was ruled illegal to reproduce a program contained within a ROM. The judgement was based partly upon the fact that the defendant had caused the program to be displayed on a visual display unit and had then copied it to produce a new ROM. There have been amendments to the law in the 1980s but the author's exclusive rights to ROM and other forms of software remain doubtful. Fortunately source programs are protected.

10.4 Patent law

The patent law in Britain has long historical roots originating in the massive trade expansion that occurred in the earlier part of the fifteenth century. As a consequence, a well-defined procedure has evolved in which there is a contract between (1) the individual inventor, and (2) the state. The inventor provides information concerning the invention and the information is made public. In return, the inventor is given a monopoly on the use of the invention. The monopoly applies for many years, as shown in table 10.2. The objectives of patent are

(1) at an individual level, to encourage inventors to be productive and to encourage inventors to use their ideas in the market place without fear of their inventions being stolen
(2) at a state level, to reduce duplication of effort and so increase national progress and prosperity.

Over the past decade, despite the fact that there has been little or no protection of software under patent law in Britain, there is little evidence to show that inventors have been unwilling to develop software. American experience is similar. This appears to confound the theory that without patent protection, innovation will be held back (Tapper, 1982).

Patent law in Britain rests on five requirements, which are

(1) novelty: it is not possible to patent an object that in any way simply reflects the current state of the art.
(2) inventive step: an invention must not be obvious to any party who is skilled in the application area.
(3) industrial application: an invention must be such that it can be seen to have industrial application.
(4) disclosure of invention: the patent specification must be sufficiently clear and complete for another skilled person to be able to recreate the invention.
(5) patentability: under the current legislation of the Patent Act 1977, certain things cannot be patented; these include discoveries, scientific theories and mathematical methods; computer programs are specifically excluded.

In Britain, the Patent office issued a note in 1969 stating that a program could not be patented. Later, the Banks Committee recommended that all programs be excluded from patentability where the inventive step lay in the program itself and referred to the example of a computer-controlled steel plant being patentable as an invention if the invention did not reside simply in details of the program (Cmnd 4407, 1970). Subsequently, for the first time under United Kingdom law, computer programs were provided for explicitly.

Under the Patent Act 1977, computer programs are excluded. This conforms to the obligations created by European patent legislation. Nevertheless, a patent application related to a computer program can succeed if the program is part of an industrial process. Under this legislation it is apparent that there will be only a small number of applications for computer programs to be patented and the number of patents accepted that incorporate a computer program will be severely limited.

In the USA, the evolution of patent law practice has been somewhat tortuous and certainly different from that in the United Kingdom. In 1968, the American Patent Office excluded all programs, but in 1969 it was decided that each patent application should be evaluated on its own merits on a case-by-case basis. A citation in 1971 was of particular significance because the Court of Customs and Patent Appeal decided to allow patent to a program

- for converting binary coded decimal notation to pure decimal notation, and
- for which the equipment to be used by the program was not stated.

It is perhaps not surprising that this decision was soon reversed by the Supreme Court.

In more recent cases, there has been agreement between the Supreme Court and the Patent Office. In 1978, the Supreme Court supported the Patent Office, against the Federal Court, and refused patent on a computer program method for calculating alarm limit values in an industrial chemical process; the program was judged to be within the state of the art. It has been suggested (Stern, 1978) that the Court was concerned to prevent abstract principles being monopolised because abstract principles are the essential tools of technology. By contrast, in 1981 the Supreme Court supported the granting of a patent for an industrial process that incorporated a computer program (Hayhurst, 1982).

Another interesting citation is that of Valport which has taken virtually a decade to resolve. In 1982, a patent was granted for the financial package Valport. The patent related to a method of operating a computer on which the system Valport runs, rather than the simple program (Enticknap, 1982). Valport calculates the value of a securities portfolio. It takes shareholdings of a portfolio and multiplies each shareholding by latest market price to give valuation. Valport is not marketed as a package but as a timesharing service with a database of over 60,000 securities. More than ten different types of report can be generated from the database and the service is available through a terminal using a dial-up connection. Therefore, the patent applies to a total system for valuation of a securities' portfolio and provides a service to many simultaneous users who access a database which is updated daily. Will similar general purpose package systems be granted patent in the future?

In the USA the decisions and decision reversals have not made the task of patent claimants or examiners any easier and Tapper suggests that opinions as to patentability "must rest on the interpretation of the oracular pronouncements of the Supreme Court and minute examination of the entrails of particular decisions." Nevertheless, it appears that patent applications in the USA will fail if an algorithm is to be patented but may succeed if a program is part of an invention that creates an industrial process. Thus despite its different gestation, in operation the present patent law in the USA is not greatly dissimilar to that in the United Kingdom.

10.5 Trade secrets and confidentiality

The common law relating to trade secrets and confidentiality has the advantage of being adaptable to new technologies and new circumstances. Unfortunately its evolution over short time-periods is somewhat haphazard. This law, which is wider than patent and copyright, can be used for the protection of computer software. For example, analysts and programmers can be restrained by contractual provision from making software available to other parties either during their period with a company or after they have ceased to be company employees. In addition, documentation such as clerical procedure manuals and data flow diagrams can also be protected.

The law of trade secret and confidentiality is restricted quite naturally to what is secret or confidential. In the United Kingdom, computer software is in principle eligible for protection under this law but there are no reported cases.

In the USA, this is the most widely used form of legal protection; this may reflect more on the inadequacy of patent and copyright law rather than on anything else. It is dissimilar to copyright and patent law in that it is non-federal. Individuals and companies can use this approach to bind themselves in contract but the common difficulty that may ensue is with third parties, not with signatorees. A contract between party A and party B does not bind a third party X unless X knowingly encourages B to break a secrecy contract with A. In such circumstances, X can buy from B a machine that includes a ROM built and created by A, and unload the ROM with impunity. If the selling of equipment by B to X is in breach of the contract between A and B, then A will still not have rights against X.

10.6 International cooperation and copyright reform

Patent, copyright and trade secret laws have been evolved for specific situations and not for computer software, as illustrated in table 10.2. It is apparent that patent although appropriate for a concrete product is ill-fitted for information; that copyright is suitable for protection against copying of word combinations, drawings and apparently software but will give little protection against unauthorised use of programs; and that trade secret and contract law is uncertain in its scope especially with respect to parties outside of the contract.

A result of the general dissatisfaction with current law is a demand for new law

Table 10.3   Period of copyright in different countries in Europe

Country	Term of protection is life of author plus that period shown below
Germany and Austria	70 years
France, the Netherlands and Gt Britain	50 years
U.S.S.R. and Malta	25 years
Albania	Life of surviving spouse plus period during which any of the author's children are under 25 years of age

to provide for the special problems of software. The options proposed vary from minor modifications of existing law to special drafted software law. One method is through the extensive use of patent law but only on payment of a high fee. This would deter all but the most serious claims. It involves significant discrimination in favour of wealthy companies and as such is unacceptable. Another suggestion is the registration of software. The owner registers (a) a copy of the program and (b) a description of the concepts used in the program. The registrar publishes the description of concepts immediately but the program remains secret for ten years. The fee involved is nominal because the procedure involves little or no examination by the registrar. The method was proposed by IBM in 1968 and is intended for use with large programs which are too obvious for patent. The registration would protect against unauthorised copying. However it would be quite legal to refer to the published concepts and then to develop a similar program to that registered. A weakness of this proposal is that it might be very difficult to prove whether program instructions have been developed independently or copied.

It has been suggested that the best way forward is to harmonise copyright laws worldwide. This is difficult to achieve even across Europe because there are many problems. For example, the period of protection varies across the continent with the result that a work may be in copyright in one country and at the same time out of copyright elsewhere. This is illustrated in table 10.3. However, a greater problem is the philosophical basis of copyright law which in many countries is fundamentally different from that in the USA and in the United Kingdom. In general, copyright in Europe is considered as an individual right coming from the author's soul, whereas in the United Kingdom it is nothing more than an economic right. Consequently, authors in European countries (outside of Britain) have rights in copyrighted work that transcend sales to publishers. It is these additional rights that delay harmonisation efforts.

There has been long and active consideration all over the world to reform this area, including efforts by the World Intellectual Property Organisation (WIPO) in Geneva (WIPO, 1978). In the summer of 1983, a meeting of delegates from governments and international organisations was organised by WIPO. The meeting considered a draft treaty aimed specifically at copyright protection of software. Although it would have taken some 5 years to have become ratified and operative worldwide, the treaty proposals were significant because they covered

- unauthorised use of software
- copying of software
- development of software that is substantially similar to other companies' products.

The organisation WIPO recommended that the law, one specifically for software which goes beyond copyright legislation, be enforced internationally. This was an attempt to improve existing law and also to harmonise international copyright law. After deliberations of one week, it was concluded that the draft treaty was unacceptable and that existing national copyright laws should be used for software protection. The difficulty with this approach is that different countries are at different stages in their introduction of software copyright protection. West Germany, the USA and Hungary have similar copyright legislation specifically related to software. Many other nations have little or no suitable rules (McLening, 1983).

Although no final conclusion has been reached, it appears that there is a consensus in favour of (1) protection of software, and (2) using something akin to copyright for protection, with the question of registration unresolved. This position is supported by the recommendations outlined in table 10.4. These recommendations were the outcome of discussions of two Specialist Groups of the British Computer Society (Grover and Hart, 1982) in response to the government Green Paper (Cmnd 8302, 1981).

Table 10.4   Recommendations made at a meeting of two Specialist Groups of the British Computer Society in October, 1981 (Grover and Hart, 1982)

(1) Urgent action is required to protect computer software
(2) A program produced at a terminal and held in store should be considered to be reduced to material form
(3) Conversion of an original work realised as a magnetic recording to electronic or other realisations of a machine code should be considered as an adaptation of the original work
(4) No distinction should be made between a display on a VDU and hard copy printout (there was dissent on this point)
(5) Any form of copying, however transient, should be a copyright infringement
(6) That the Society be asked to endorse in particular the proposal that alternative expressions of the original program should fall within the definition of adaptation and so lie within the copyright of the program

10.7 Protection by technical contrivance

In many situations, legal protection may be complemented by technical means. These include use of manufacturer's protection utilities, purpose built hardware devices, locks within the software and use of cryptography.

Manufacturers of microcomputers advise their users of methods for software protection. Typical diskette protection schemes are changed address headers, changed alignment of the tracks, adjusting the speed of the disk drive to affect the count of bytes on a track or combinations of these schemes (Apple, 1982). In the more relevant and common situation of a software supplier providing programs to another organisation, the manufacturer's protection methods are of limited value. Consequently, the supplier will use other methods such as the provision of software in machine readable object code. For valuable software, additional protection is necessary such as that provided by special hardware mechanisms. One device is a dongle which is attached to the appropriate user port of the microcomputer. A dongle contains unique coding which is interrogated by the program when a program is loaded. It allows backup copies of software to be made but a copy program cannot be run on another machine unless the machine has a dongle. The device locks a package into selected machines but thereby limits portability. Another hardware device to prevent illicit copying has been devised by Adi Shamir. The device alters the disk drive so that any attempt to copy software will cause a machine crash.

Another approach is to use copy-protect means which deter thieves rather than preventing theft. An encrypted version of the user's name is inserted at specific points within the software. For example, software distributed by dealers may have both the dealer's name and the user's name encrypted and added to the package program which is on diskette. If the software is copied, the two names will appear on all screen and hardcopy output reports. Date and count locks may be advantageous by causing the software to cease to run after a specific number of runs or after a certain date. Another method is to personalise the source code through the inclusion of redundant but recognisable sections of code. This may enable a piece of programming, suspected as being stolen, to be identified as the work of a particular programmer. The identifiable code may take the form of a harmless bug or an unusual way of achieving a result.

Generally, technical safeguards are not perfect and a determined professional thief can identify the traps and immobilise or bypass them. Even a dongle can be circumvented by finding and excising the instructions in the program that test for the presence of the device; or by writing a routine that simulates the dongle operation. Therefore, it may be desirable in some cases to use cryptography. One method under development uses a public-key cryptosystem (Rivest *et al.*, 1978). The only problem is that of hiding the private deciphering key, because there is nowhere on a floppy disk where the private key can be hidden from the skilled professional. The key is safer inside a physically tamper-proof box.

Technical safeguards deter the amateur copier. The professional pirate will in time circumvent most safeguards. Cryptosystems offer the best protection (Maude and Maude, 1984).

10.8 Conclusions

Software is not completely protectable under present-day law. Patents, trade secret laws and copyrights can be used to some degree. However, infringement can be difficult to detect and unless a third party markets a similar product, it is not possible to guarantee that software is safe, even with steel-clad legal protection.

Patenting of software is inherently controversial and has divided legal commentators. Nevertheless, the legal profession appears to share the opinion that software, isolated from machinery invention, should not be patentable. Trade secret law provides wider scope but is restricted to apply to that which can be shown to be confidential. A major advantage of copyright is that it intimidates users of proprietary software from indiscriminate copying. Copyright law as it stands is not effective but there are many who believe that copyright or its derivatives offer the best mechanism for legal protection.

Advances in technology may lead to virtually pirate-proof software. Unfortunately, current technical devices and existing law cannot guarantee protection. Therefore, the best software must use safeguards that incorporate many disincentives, deterrents and physical protection features. A government Green Paper in 1983 said "A nation such as the United Kingdom relies heavily on getting value from its intellectual property. . . we have a tradition of world-leading inventions. The ability to claim ownership of ideas is a vital step in securing a profit from them." Software is currency; it is essential that those who provide the currency are protected from counterfeiting and duplicity.

Questions

10.1 A software protection mechanism could be based upon patent law with a very small registration fee and a relatively shorter period of protection. What are the difficulties with this method?

10.2 Proposed legislation in Japan may provide protection for only fifteen years and this may discourage collaborative ventures with Western software houses. Discuss.

10.3 With the development of good technical safeguards for protecting proprietary software, there will be no need for legislation to protect software. Discuss.

11 Illustrative Examples of Breaches of Security

In this chapter a number of incidents from real-life are cited, not as criticisms of the organisations in which the incidents occurred but as an attempt to assist future innovators of information systems to avoid some of the difficulties which all too often have arisen in the past.

A privacy incident is outlined to provide a better understanding of the pressure that has been exerted on governments to legislate for data protection. A company that had its computer destroyed shows the benefits of contingency planning.

The other four incidents are selected because they demonstrate the critical place that human components have in information systems. In each of the four cases there was a failure — that is, the information system behaved in an unacceptable manner which was unforeseen by the system designer. In each case it was the human component that failed. Sometimes it was the user of the system who was at fault and on other occasions it was the computer professional who behaved irregularly. This is not meant to imply that it is easy to identify people who are likely to behave abnormally and therefore are unsuited to work in, or with, information systems. No, it is quite the reverse. In fact, one of the remarkable features of crime and insecurity related to computer based information systems is the strange range of people involved and the misdemeanant is generally a first-time offender. This has repercussions for the company personnel officer who is required to give an opinion on prospective employees. All the incidents highlight the importance of company policies in computing, including company contingency planning, company internal controls, recruitment procedures and policy on use of computer resources by data processing staff.

11.1 A privacy incident

This incident, which was reported on a BBC *Panorama* programme (BBC, 1981), concerns an industrial film maker who innocently became involved in a Kafkaesque intelligence gathering nightmare.

A film maker joined a company which specialised in making films for industrial clients. Shortly after taking up this new appointment, her employer informed her that there was a serious problem because a client, a major British construction company, had indicated that she, the film maker, was a security risk. The company stated that she would not be welcome on its premises and that it would not allow her to work on its assignment.

The film maker was absolutely shattered. Despite considerable efforts she and her employer were unable to establish the reasons for her being a security risk. As a result she thought that her career might be ruined and that she might never be able to work again professionally, because if one company could obtain information about her then other companies could do the same. Consequently, the victim and her husband gave thought to moving north and to opening a restaurant or other activity in which nobody would think it necessary to check on her background. The film maker's predicament was horrific but unlike other possible victims she had two patrons with considerable influence who were able to unravel the mystery.

The first patron was her employer, a former renowned BBC broadcaster. He was unwilling to accept a simple refusal from the client company. He insisted on knowing the source of the information which stated that his employee was a security risk. A link with the Security Branch was established. There are over one-thousand Special Branch officers in the United Kingdom. The Special Branch has its London headquarters at Scotland Yard. It has many tasks but its most delicate activity is that of domestic surveillance of people involved in offences against the security of the state. This role extends to maintaining political files on citizens. The Special Branch, because of its role, often gives the impression of being a central agency somewhat similar to the CIA in the USA. This is not correct. Special Branch officers are part of the CID, the Criminal Investigation Department, and as such are part of the police force.

The film maker's second patron was her father, who was a retired senior officer from Scotland Yard. He was able to make contact with the Special Branch through his ex-colleagues in the police. It became evident that the starting point of the nightmare was a shooting incident with the Baader-Meinhoff terrorists in Amsterdam. As a result the police in the Netherlands were in a state of alert and at that time the film maker and her husband travelled through the Netherlands at the start of a holiday. The couple arrived at a café for refreshments looking rather bedraggled and tired because they had spent a night on the car ferry from England. It appears that the waiter was suspicious and thought that the husband resembled Willie Stoller, a Baader–Meinhoff terrorist. The local police were contacted and information was passed to the police regarding the Renault car in which the tourists were travelling. The assistance of the Special Branch in London was requested. The car was registered in the wife's name. Enquiries were made about the wife, not about the husband. The enquiries, in the sense of establishing a terrorist link, were fruitless. The Special Branch did not proceed further with the enquiry. The film maker was not interviewed and continued on her holiday without ever knowing or suspecting that her name had been under consideration by the Special Branch. Unfortunately, the basic details remained on Special Branch files.

After the incident had been resolved, the innocent party asked a Special Branch officer what would have happened to her if her father had not been able to use his position of influence to make contact with the Special Branch and instead she had been forced to use a lawyer. She said that she was told that no details would have been released. The result would have been that the innocent party would have had her career ruined and spent the rest of her life as a security risk because of one mistake by one officer.

11.2 Non-computer personnel and insecurity of information systems

It is not necessary to have vast knowledge of computers to use computers for fraudulent purposes. In the following incidents, the perpetrators were highly respected clerical staff who regularly used computer based systems in their work. As is common with white-collar crime, the offenders were first-time offenders who took advantage of opportunities created by the victims, namely their employers. The two incidents provide evidence that it is not the case that crime is committed by a small group of people who can easily be distinguished from the main group of law-abiding citizens.

11.2.1 A user instructs an information system to make fraudulent payments

The supervisor of the payments department in a local authority in London found a method of creating false documents, entering them into the system and concealing the inputs. These false entries resulted in three cheques worth £13,956 being paid to 'David Allen' which was an alias of the supervisor's son. The son collected the money and paid £2000 into his mother's building society account; the account used the false name of 'Barbara White' but the supervisor's own address.

An internal auditor was completing a routine check of actual expenditure against budget and purely by accident discovered two cheques which he could not explain. As a result an investigation started. On hearing of the investigation the supervisor asked for the balance in the account of 'Barbara White' to be sent to her address as a cheque; she returned the envelope unopened to the building society after writing across the envelope 'not known at this address'. Unfortunately this did not convince the judge when the case was heard in 1982 at the Central Criminal Court in London — a trial which newspapers described as the first case of computer fraud to be tried at the Old Bailey, even though in fact in the 1970s there had been earlier computer fraud trials.

The son, who had used several thousand pounds on visits to Australia and Canada, pleaded guilty to the charge of conspiracy to defraud but his mother denied the charge. The supervisor was found guilty and was jailed for twelve months.

11.2.2 Executive officer uses salaries system to defraud health authority

This incident occurred in the paymaster's department of a health authority where expenses incurred by doctors were normally paid at the end of each month with the monthly salary payment. However, there was a facility to pay expenses separately via another system, quite independent of the main payroll system — presumably for special cases and for speedy payments. One of the payclerks took advantage of this situation. In general, doctors' expenses were paid by means of the main payroll system. On some occasions, the payclerk not only put an expenses claim through the main system but she also used the secondary system to make a duplicate payment of the same expenses claim with a hand-issued cheque going to the payclerk direct (Lane and Wright, 1979).

In December 1977 after some £13,000 had been stolen, the malpractice was discovered when the clerk was absent because of sickness. A kidney specialist asked for payment of a £425 claim which he had submitted earlier in the month; he was unaware that it had been arranged to pay this with his monthly salary. This apparently straightforward request brought to light the fact that the expenses had already been paid through the secondary system and that the hand-issued cheque had gone astray.

The frauds were carried out over two years during which the clerk had been promoted because of her expertise, diligence and reliability. The payclerk pleaded guilty to thirteen fraud charges and was jailed for a year at Winchester Crown Court.

11.3 Mis-use of computer in an insurance company

This security breach occurred in an insurance company of international repute based in the United Kingdom (Samocuik, 1982). In 1981, the company's premium income exceeded £400 million and to support this operation it used a large IBM/3033 computer system with online terminal facilities to company offices in South Africa, the USA and the United Kingdom. The procedure for accessing the computer was to switch on the terminal and to press the return key, to which the system would respond with a request for the terminal user to indicate which application system or other service the user wished to activate, followed by a signing-on key and password. Signing-on keys were allocated locally by management but the password was selected by a user to prevent illegal use of resources by an intruder who had illegally obtained a signing-on key. Programmers were able to enter, sort, retrieve and save data; and inspect and modify files through a powerful and widely used online development system, ROSCOE, supplied by Applied Data Research of Princeton in the USA. The data processing department, based in the provinces, had responsibility for developing and maintaining software and for providing general data processing services.

A senior systems analyst who had worked for the company for twelve years and who considered himself to be a loyal, hardworking employee, was on holiday at a time during which a programmer accidentally listed some files and programs in the ROSCOE library. Subsequently, a senior manager authorised an investigation, discovering programs for personal accounting purposes and for gambling on football pools programs which had been used twenty-five and forty-three times respectively. The analyst was dismissed but later in December 1981 with the support of his staff association he appealed to an industrial tribunal held in Gloucester on the grounds that (a) the application software had never been used for business purposes, as the accounting for his girlfriend's company to which the software related was done manually because the volume of entries was small as the business was part-time and run merely to supplement his girlfriend's income as a teacher, (b) the computer was widely abused by staff and (c) after his dismissal another employee who had been discovered mis-applying computer resources had only been suspended and after two weeks reinstated. The dismissal of the systems analyst was ruled fair by the tribunal and no compensation was granted.

As a result of the tribunal hearing, *Computer Fraud and Security Bulletin* investigated and completed an in-depth analysis of the events and reported "a much more serious state of affairs . . ." with "gross deficiencies in computer security." The employee who had only been suspended was not employed by the data processing department but was an information analyst in London with the planning and research department concerned with analysing business trends and preparing statistics. He had been with the company for five years but prior to that had had wide computing experience including a period as a software programmer. He knew about the system ROSCOE and in particular about the very powerful and comprehensive facilities it provides for the management of the terminal services; these facilities should be available only to authorised staff under rigorous control.

In the period prior to the tribunal hearings, the data processing department reviewed the system logs and discovered that a remote user had illegally accessed the chief programmer's personal library. The user was identified and was found to have a program that totally bypassed the security controls and listed the contents of any part of the development library — a finding that caused a major panic because it held information of a very sensitive nature available to a small number of authorised users. The program belonged to the information analyst who worked for supervisors who did not have the technical knowledge to spot what the analyst was doing. If the analyst had known or wished to, he could have accessed an evaluation program for the grading of senior management on a points basis — if the data and criteria had been released the personnel department would have been acutely embarassed. It would also have been possible to accumulate information relating to insurance brokers, calculation of premiums and marketing statistics — information that is valuable to a competitor. Even more significantly, with additional knowledge he had acquired about an IBM-standard utility SUPERZAP, the analyst had the capability to remove evidence of system use from the system log. Whereas the investigation into the behaviour of the systems analyst was carried out openly and vigorously resulting in "a compre-hensive dossier of his misdeeds," the investigation into the information analyst was done with relative secrecy. The information analyst pleaded that he had used his expertise only to gain a better service for his department by changing department priority ratings for processing of his work and as a result was given a formal warning for gross misconduct with suspension for two weeks on full pay. The incident with the information analyst, unlike the one with the systems analyst, received little or no attention from the press.

11.4 Computer personnel steal files and demand ransom

An operations manager and a systems analyst worked for ICI on an IBM 370/145 system at Rosenberg, the Netherlands which had a backup site at Wynhaven. The operations manager was reviewing security procedures with the intention of improving security and realised that there was a major weakness in the existing procedures because one person, the operations manager himself, had access to the main data library and the backup stores. Collusion was unnecessary and the operations manager had simply to sign authorisation requests to withdraw the master and backup files from the two locations. The manager did use an accomplice but only in order to identify which files to take and to provide specific software expertise.

The accomplices stole master files and backup copies in the form of forty-eight disk packs and over five-hundred tapes which together held major data of the company (Lane and Wright, 1979). The media were hidden in Antwerp in an air-conditioned apartment selected for its suitability for storing magnetic media. Then the partners in crime demanded £275,000 for the return of the files and threatened to destroy the files if the ransom was not paid. Although they were competent computer personnel, they were less than competent as criminals in that they were poor at collecting the ransom.

They telephoned a senior executive who had been at an earlier time the superior of the operations manager and instructed him to get the money and deliver it to them in London in the form of used £5 and £10 notes. To show that they were serious they forwarded one tape, from which they had partly erased the data, together with an audio-cassette message. The message made it clear what they had done to the tape and indicated that they would destroy the files if their demands were not met. The company valued the data at £150,000 and thought that it would require some six man-years to re-create the data. The accomplices attempted to arrange a meeting in Oxford Street, London, but the meeting was unsuccessful. As the company executive was leaving, the pair arrived on a scooter; they attempted to snatch a bag carried by the executive believing that the bag contained the money. They were arrested after a chase and wrestle which was described in the computer press as a Keystone Kops' chase.

While awaiting trial and on bail, the operations manager was able to obtain contract work in a number of computer installations; he used his own name and was dismissed only when he told employers about his connection with the ICI affair. The operations manager and the systems analyst were sentenced to six years and five years, respectively — sentences which were reduced to four years and three years on appeal.

11.5 Boiler explosion destroys computer office suite

A company in Kent, England, had the misfortune to have its computer centre virtually completely destroyed in August 1977 (Norman, 1983). The incident is illustrated in figure 11.1.

In the early hours of the morning, the boiler's control equipment malfunctioned. There was a build up of steam which caused the boiler to explode. The boiler, situated beneath the computer centre, passed through the ceiling of the boiler room, through the data preparation area, and then out of the building through the concrete roof before coming to rest after falling through the roof of a second building six metres away.

The explosion created a six metre hole in the floor of the data preparation room. Eight direct data entry terminals and eight punch card machines were

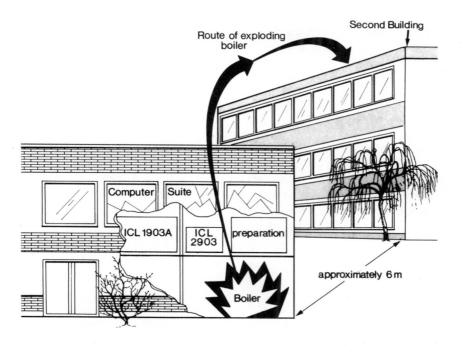

Figure 11.1 Explosion destroys computer centre

damaged because of a fall or the explosion. The company's ICL2903 computer
fell to the room below and consequently was written off. During normal activities
twenty staff worked in the area where the floor collapsed but fortunately at the
time of the explosion no staff were in the area where the main damage occurred.
Two night shift operators were working nearby on the ICL1903 system but escaped
unhurt. The ICL1903 computer was covered in dust and water sludge and although
not destroyed was out of action temporarily.

Many magnetic tapes and disks in and near the damaged area were destroyed
but the company was fortunate to have backup files stored away from the computer
suite. Therefore to restore processing services it was necessary to find only alternative computer power. The computer manufacturer assisted the company to find
a user some 85 kilometres away with sufficient computer capacity to process
extra data. Three days after the explosion, six operators moved into hotel accom-
modation near the site of the temporary computer to enable processing to resume.
Data were transported between the company and the temporary computer using
a helicopter.

The old computer suite was unsafe and it was necessary to provide new accom-
modation. It took fifteen days from the time of the incident to prepare a new
computer suite and to bring processing back to normal. The damaged ICL1903
system was restored and an ICL1902T system replaced the destroyed computer.
The backup files plus extra finance and a little extra effort vere sufficient to
retrieve the situation.

Misfortune did not become calamity because of the contingency plans of the
company.

11.6 Case study lessons

The case studies are examples of problems that can occur with computer based
information systems. They are not cited so that others can look at the failures
to say how virtuous they themselves are; because this is just too easy and, as
Americans say, "hindsight is always 20/20 vision;" but they are quoted to enable
organisations, managers, users and information system designers to avoid the
misadventures experienced by others.

11.6.1 Privacy incident

The privacy incident acts as a note of caution for designers of information systems
because it emphasises that human components of systems do not always behave
in a predictable manner. The police have a tradition of discipline and yet on that

occasion a police officer made a serious mistake and did something that cannot be explained. It is reasonable to assume that people in ordinary civilian businesses will on occasion also behave unpredictably, causing abnormal system behaviour. Although the system used by the police at that time was not computer based, the events show the sort of damage that can be created by dissemination of incorrect information. The case emphasises the need for effective data protection legislation and, with respect to current legislation in the United Kingdom, it adds support to the argument that legislation that does not include manual systems and excludes police systems is suspect (Gostin, 1984). An intriguing point which remains unresolved is the procedure by which the construction company obtained access to Special Branch files holding confidential personal data that were not accessible to the data subject. It is hoped that legislation will at least eliminate this type of absurdity. Last but not least are the lessons from this incident which can be learned by designers of information systems who are required to take cognisance of the frailty of humans while designing systems that will operate within the law.

11.6.2 Theft of magnetic media

The two twenty-seven-year-old computer professionals, employed by ICI, were the first people in the world to be convicted on charges of stealing vital computer disk and tape media from their employers and demanding ransom money. The case highlights faults that existed in the company's procedures — faults that the operations manager was employed to spot and correct. At that time, few managers of computer installations could honestly claim that similar events were not possible in their installations. To eliminate the possibility of this type of security breach, organisations should

- ensure that access to important files is not in the hands of one member of staff, irrespective of the seniority of that one person, as it must not be assumed that those in more senior posts are more likely to resist temptation
- ensure that collusion between a number of people would be a prerequisite for media to be removed
- hold a number of generations of data files, possibly three generations, with each generation held at a different location, and with no one person having authority to remove files from all sites
- take up references for all prospective employees, including specific security checks where appropriate.

11.6.3 Incidents involving non-computer personnel

In many situations, security is dependent on the goodwill of employees rather than on the exactness of the security safeguards. Nevertheless, there can be no excuse for ignoring principles that have been developed by the accounting profession over the last century. This was the main mistake in the two case studies involving non-computer personnel. If organisations have

- clear lines of responsibilities for staff with appropriate segregation of duties
- staff employed on different functions working in different offices or different parts of the same office in order to discourage collusion between staff from different functions
- appreciation of the considerable dangers inherent in dual payment procedures
- properly maintained reconciliation and control accounts

then the temptations that were placed before the two erring users would have been minimised and the crimes probably not committed.

11.6.4 Misuse of computer resources

It is not easy to estimate precisely the size or frequency of the misuse of computer resources but published statistics for the 1970s collected by the National Computing Centre (Squires, 1980) give a similar impression to those published by the Local Government Audit Inspectorate for a five-year period beginning in 1976 (Kimmance, 1981). The former study reported only 2 incidents of unauthorised use in 142 respondents. The Audit Inspectorate's study, based on 319 respondents, as illustrated in table 11.1, reported twelve incidents of private work, representing a total loss of some £16,000, and two incidents of theft of timesharing resources, valued at approximately £500. Although the two studies indicate a relatively low level of misuse of computer resources, the actual level of misuse — as compared with the reported level — must be higher. As illustrated in the insurance company case study in section 11.3, companies, especially in the financial sector, are not always anxious to report security breaches because shareholders might be alarmed by reports of computer installation insecurity. As for the insurance company incident itself, there are many actions that can be taken to reduce the risks (Samocuik, 1982). These include

(1) establishing a company policy relating to the private use of computer resources
(2) ensuring that staff are aware of this policy and the disciplinary action that they face if they break the rules
(3) restricting the access to and the use of powerful utilities similar to SUPERZAP in ways consistent with the recommendations of the manufacturer supplier
(4) ensuring that system logs are not only written but are monitored routinely and frequently.

This last point is probably the most important of all. The insurance company incident is a perfect example of the danger of dependence on technical controls

alone — passwords and cryptography — while ignoring completely the need for
monitoring. Unfortunately, it is all too common for computer technocrats to
ignore powerful, simple, manual based safeguards in favour of protection
mechanisms that are technically sophisticated. The incident in which a company
had its computer destroyed by an explosion illustrates the benefits that can
accrue from apparently simple but effective company policies.

11.6.5 Computer fraud surveys

It is difficult to obtain access to information relating to actual computer misuse
because of the natural reluctance of organisations to provide information that
might be seen as evidence of management failure to exercise proper control.
To assess the risk from computer misuse, the Audit Inspectorate completed in
1981 its first survey of computer fraud in the United Kingdom (Kimmance, 1981).
In 1984 the Inspectorate's successor body, the Audit Commission, completed a
second survey (Audit Commission, 1985). Data from the two surveys, which are
based upon replies from public and private sector users, are shown in tables 11.1,
11.2 and 11.3. One conclusion from the surveys is that 'none of the cases appeared
to demonstrate ingenious application of technological skills: indeed the majority
took advantage of inherent weaknesses in particular procedures.'
    A second conclusion, as illustrated in table 11.3, is that over one third of the
reported incidents were undetected by routine control procedures. Although
organisations are becoming more security conscious, it must be of concern to all
computer professionals that a high number of computer security breaches appear
to be discovered by accident. This suggests that for many computer installations
security is dependent to a large degree on the honesty of personnel. Therefore, it
is essential that companies develop precise and comprehensive security policies

Table 11.1   Incidents involving theft and misuse of computer resources
as given in the computer fraud surveys of the Audit Inspectorate
and the Audit Commission

	1981 Survey covering 5 year period 319 respondents		1984 Survey covering 5 year period 943 respondents	
Fraudulent activity	*Number of incidents*	*Total loss*	*Number of incidents*	*Total loss*
Private work	12	£16,339	11	£2220
Theft of timesharing	2	£500	1	£71
Theft of software	2	£500	—	—
Theft of output	2	£40	2	—
Sabotage	3	—	3	—
Invasion of privacy	1	—	—	—
Total	22	£17,379	17	£2291

Table 11.2   Types of fraudulent activity

	1981 Survey		1984 Survey	
Fraudulent activity	*Number of incidents*	*Total loss*	*Number of incidents*	*Total loss*
Unauthorised alteration of input	42	£858,170	58	£901,001
Destruction, suppression or misappropriation of output	2	£3,600	2	£230,185
Theft or alteration of master file	1	£26,000	–	–
Theft or misuse of computer resources	22	£17,379	17	£2,301
Total	67	£905,149	77	£1,133,487

Table 11.3   Method of discovery of fraudulent activity

	1981 Survey		1984 Survey	
Discovered by	*Number of incidents*	*Proportion (per cent)*	*Number of incidents*	*Proportion (per cent)*
Internal control	28	42	40	52
Internal audit	4	6	9	12
External audit	1	1	–	–
Other means	34	51	23	30
Not disclosed	–	–	5	6
Total	67	100	77	100

related to information systems. Since computers and the information that they hold are valuable assets, they must be protected with the same care and attention as a bank safe but this is no easy task. The case studies put into dramatic perspective the significance of computer based information systems, the power that they give to those who know how the systems work and the daunting responsibility borne by the computer professionals who design information systems.

Questions

11.1 "How can we motivate highly independent, creative and often anti-authoritarian technocrats to comply with security and control procedures?" (*Computer Fraud and Security Bulletin*). Discuss.

11.2 The information analyst of the insurance company case study said that he cracked the security system simply as an intellectual exercise. "This can be compared to a person who is discovered in the bank vault on Sunday morning with a forged master key, and claims that the whole exercise was carried out as an intellectual challenge." (*Computer Fraud and Security Bulletin*). Discuss.

11.3 It must concern management that such a high number of cases of computer insecurity seems to have been discovered by accident. Discuss.

11.4 After reading the insurance company case study, a student said that he thought that the dismissal of the systems analyst was unjust because the analyst simply used a machine that was idle — at least the spare capacity was idle — and consequently there was no additional cost to the employer. Therefore he should not have been punished. Discuss.

11.5 A computer manufacturer says "We are not prepared to spend further resources on increasing security features until users demand that we do so. Security does not sell systems." (*Computer Fraud and Security Bulletin*). Discuss.

12 Postscript

Over the last 20 years the computer scene has been one of continual change. As the information age progresses, more changes and important developments in information technology will cause organisations, both small and large, to automate functions previously done manually. Consequently, valuable company assets, some virtually irreplaceable, will be added to those assets that are currently held and represented in electronic form. From a security point of view, this wider use of information technology in business operations implies greater vulnerability to threats. The threats include those from white-collar criminals which can result in losses from theft, embezzlement, fraud and sabotage. The increased dangers, combined with an evolving and expanding use of information technology, create an environment in which

- there is greater need for trustworthy and security-conscious employees
- there are new forms of assets which may be subject to threat with opportunity for misdemeanants to use new methods of attack
- the time-scale for security breaches changes from weeks or days to seconds or nano-seconds
- a security breach is not specific to one geographical location but may be executed through a communications network from a place that may be miles or even thousands of miles from the actual scene of the incident.

If the above scenario is superimposed upon the present business situation, in which a high proportion of losses occur because of accidental, as opposed to deliberate, events, it is reasonable to assume that in the future there will be

- an increase in the number of security failures because of the greater number of computers and the wider use of information technology in business operations
- new applications of information technology, which will create additional vulnerabilities and provide new mechanisms for perpetrating computer based crimes — for example, electronic funds transfer systems move millions of pounds each day within the United Kingdom and internationally and a breach of this type of system provides opportunity for rapid laundering of money as well as for fraud

- substantial increase in the size of loss resulting from significant breaches of security (Parker, *et al.*, 1984).

To overcome or to neutralise these problems, an organisation should have a company plan for security which recognises the need for qualitative judgements and a systems approach.

12.1 A company plan

Historically, computing has been regarded as benign, that is without evil intent. This is unrealistic. Nowadays, the potential for misdemeanour and for accidental misfortune is widely recognised and the need for security understood, especially as highly sensitive and invaluable personal data and data representing millions of pounds are on the move electronically every day. In military systems, threats come from sophisticated technical attack and from people. The response is to commit large amounts of financial and human resources to protect information. In general, the position in the business world is in marked contrast with this. The technical problem is small, if not negligible, and the main threat to a computer based information system is from personnel who are authorised to work with the system and consequently know the ways to exploit it. This may change in the future but at present there are many technical mechanisms and administrative and procedural controls that can deter would-be offenders, and the real dangers to business systems stem not from the vulnerabilities of the protection mechanisms but from the absence of company commitment to place security of information on the same level of importance as that given to the protection of other valuable corporate assets. This is illustrated by a recent survey (Datapro, 1985) of over one-thousand installations which found that over half have no disaster plan and that nearly a quarter do not intend to develop a plan.

12.2 Qualitative judgements and a systems approach

The safeguards required to protect an information system against misuse by an intelligent adversary must be as varied and comprehensive as the possible attacks — an example of the law of requisite variety (Ashby, 1976). Although this is difficult to achieve, a company that is committed to defend its information systems can formulate and implement an appropriate, complex and integrated defence plan, incorporating technical, administrative and organisational measures. In the process of developing countermeasures, quantitative analysis may be meaningful but in many aspects of security there is need for a complex balancing of judgements which includes

- judgements concerning the existence of accidental and deliberate threats

   including motives and capabilities of attackers
- judgements in the estimation of the value of protected objects
- judgements related to the effectiveness of security mechanisms.

It is apparent that security is similar to many other business decisions in that it involves risk taking based on qualitative judgements.

In problems of this nature, many people should participate, as described in chapter 8. Methods that support this are peer reviews, scenario analysis, participative design (Land, 1982), and the Checkland methodology. Security demands a holistic approach. In fact, there can be no subject in computing that exhibits a stronger case than security for a systems approach, such as the formalised method of Checkland for organisational learning.

12.3 Microcomputers

During the last few years, there has been massive growth in the number of microcomputers used by organisations, in many cases by first-time users. The innovation and growth have brought many benefits — the most significant being that microcomputers have made computing very popular and have motivated non-computer personnel to become users. Microcomputers are portable, which in itself is a great advantage, but portability coupled with genuine timesharing capability and hands-on facility has made computing readily available in every small office throughout the world of business and commerce. The microcomputer, because it is portable, can be taken home to do office work. Similarly, the timesharing potential is different from the mainframe timesharing facility because each user has his or her own processor. Regrettably, few things come free of cost and many that appear free at the start incur significant cost in the end. Microcomputers are no exception and one cost or disadvantage is that security procedures and good practices, which have taken a decade to evolve for mainframe computers, are being ignored or undermined. In general, users of microcomputers do not realise the dangers inherent in computing and believe that the only dangers are theft of hardware and software. This ignores the fact that (1) information stored on floppy disks may be considerably more valuable than the machine itself and (2) the majority of security problems that are discussed throughout this book apply not only to mainframes but also to microcomputers. The position with respect to microcomputers is such that it is suggested that microcomputers, in security terms, have put the clock back to the 1960s (Highland, 1983). The problems that occur with microcomputers can be grouped as (1) people problems and (2) technical problems.

   One effect of microcomputers is to have fewer staff per machine. This leaves little or no opportunity for division of duties. One person may enter data, program and operate a machine. The danger is obvious. In addition, other deterrents such as audit review may be absent, because the cost of an audit is high compared with the cost of the equipment.

Technical weaknesses, as shown in table 12.1, cause a number of security problems. For example, system software developments are relatively primitive and consequently more vulnerable than the hardware. Operating system software does not provide job accounting, library and file security or terminal control — a poor security foundation for computer based information systems. Many micro-computers offer simple password protection. Naturally, the password facilities are not as sophisticated as the facilities on mainframe computers and since no log is maintained by the system, it is not easy to detect repeated unsuccessful attempts to gain access which might signify illegal penetration attempts. Therefore, to provide a stable and secure environment, local staff must police the machine area to detect and deter potential offenders. Two other areas of contention are erase commands and software utilities. Often the former do not remove data from disks but simply remove the name of the file from the disk's directory. Users must be aware of this and take other protective measures or use programs that do remove data. Utilities give power to any user to rename or remove any file. Therefore, the utilities must be available on restricted circulation to auth-orised personnel only.

Table 12.1   Vulnerabilities and controls in microcomputing

Vulnerability	*Control*
Password protection methods	Use the staff to police and so to detect and deter
Erasing dead files	Use a program that overwrites all obsolete records
Powerful software utilities	Restrict use by placing utilities outside general release
Backup copies of files not maintained	Improved training and procedures

If there is (1) organisational commitment and (2) a reasonable level of expertise, then the difficulties outlined above can be overcome. The result is a relatively secure microcomputer environment with one exception — lack of separation of duties. This is recognised by the Local Government Audit Inspectorate which suggests that the attractiveness of microcomputing will lead to the gradual elimination of one of the fundamental control safeguards, namely separation of duties (Kimmance, 1981).

12.4 A good design is a secure system

After a period during which security was considered to be of only tangential interest to the development of computer based information systems, there are now many designers and organisations who appreciate that a well-designed information system incorporates security and creates a secure system. This is not to ignore the fact that there are many organisations that do not commit adequate resources to secure their information systems and therefore appear to be unaware of the risks implicit in computing. Although it is extremely expensive, if not impossible, to achieve absolute security, in the majority of business situations it is possible to achieve high levels of security at a cost that is trivial and insignificant compared with the losses that might occur in the absence of adequate security. Security is fundamental to the design of computer based information systems but there is no simple recipe or cookbook for achieving this. As Donn Parker says "An effective method must anticipate that a game is being played and the rules of the game are made by the enemy, not the security specialist." A systems designer must therefore be as innovative as a potential offender and have a breadth of vision to equal the challenge of a wide range of difficult threats. The ideas presented in this book have attempted to illustrate the complexity and comprehensiveness of security in order to provide the designer with a thorough understanding of the problems and issues. Without a full appreciation, attempts to implement security in isolated areas may result in a total security programme being inadequate and inappropriate. An effective security programme must bring together a diverse but coherent assembly of methods and techniques which represent a reasonable balance between absolute security and user serviceability.

Questions

12.1 "There is no answer to computer fraud other than raising personal levels of integrity and responsibility so that recruits for this inviting new field of criminality are so few as not to matter." (J. Hemming, in a letter in *The Guardian*, 20 October 1983). Discuss.

12.2 We now have available excellent security methods and techniques, such as Halon fire extinguishers and cryptographic methods, that security is within our grasp. Discuss.

12.3 Select any three microcomputers to which you have access and complete the study as outlined in question **3.15**. (Group problem)

12.4 Senior management of an organisation gives support for disaster planning. A disaster occurs and management is disappointed to find that the company is unprepared even though it was thought that there was a recovery plan. Discuss where the company may have gone wrong.

12.5 You have been asked to comment on the following computer proposal particularly with respect to security.

The proposal is to install microcomputers in the offices of social workers for storing case histories that they are studying or have studied. The offices

are public authority offices and staff often change jobs and/or cases. Therefore,.it is essential that staff who are new to a particular case can draw on
information that previous officers have collected. To support this requirement, an information system on microcomputers has been identified as a
possible solution.

The social workers operate over a relatively small geographical area, in
which one social worker may know the people about whom other social
workers are carrying out investigations, but the details of one case are confidential to that social worker and the workers superiors. Information
about cases must only be released on a need-to-know basis.

The cases that are to be stored on computer relate to non-accidental
injury to children and babies.

Discuss the implications of a microcomputer solution.

References and Bibliography

Achugbue, J.D. and Chin, F.Y. (1979). The effectiveness of output modification by rounding for protection of statistical databases. *INFOR*, Vol. 17, No. 3, 209–18

Adleman, N. (1976). *Engineering Investigations in Support of Multics Security Kernal Software Development*, ESD-TR-77-17, Honeywell Information Systems Brighton, Mass.

AFIPS (1974). *System Review Manual on Security*, American Federation of Information Processing Societies, Arlington, Virginia

AFIPS (1979). *Security – Checklist for Computer Center Self Audits*, American Federation of Information Processing Societies, Arlington, Virginia

Anderson, J.P. (1972). Information security in a multi-user computer environment. In *Advances in Computers, Vol. 12* (ed. M. Rubinoff), Academic Press, New York

Apple (1982). *Copy II Plus – an Apple Disk Utility System*, Apple Computer, Inc., Portland, Oregon, chapter 4 (entitled Diskette Protection Schemes)

Ashby, R.W. (1976). *An Introduction to Cybernetics*, Methuen, London

Attanasio, C.R., Markstein, P.W. and Phillips, R.J. (1976). Penetrating our operating system – a study of VM370 integrity. *IBM Systems Journal*, Vol. 15, No. 1, 102–16

Audit Commission (1985). *Computer Fraud Survey*, HMSO, London

Baran, P. (1964). *On Distributed Communications – Security and Secrecy*, RM-3765-PR, RAND Corporation, Santa Monica, California

BBC (1981). *Transcript of Panorama Programme of 2nd March 1981*, British Broadcasting Corporation, London

Beck, L.L. (1979). *A Security Mechanism for a Statistical Database*, Department of Computer Science, Southern Methodist University, Dallas, Texas

Black, G. and Karten, H. (1983). US scuttles the pirates. *Computer Weekly*, No. 876, 1

British Computer Society (1981). *Control and Audit of Minicomputer Systems*, Heyden, London

Broadbent, D. (1979). *Contingency Planning*, NCC, Manchester

Bunyan, A. (1979). Police and national security. In *Computers, Records and the Right to Privacy* (ed. P. Hewitt), Input Two-Nine, Purley

Checkland, P. (1981). *Systems Thinking, Systems Practice*, Wiley, Chichester

Chin, F.Y. and Ozsoyoglu, G. (1980). Security of statistical bases. In *Advances in Computer Security Management, Vol. 1* (ed. T.A. Rullo), Heyden, London, 57–8

Cmnd 4407 (1970). *British Patent System* (Chairman, M.A.L. Banks), HMSO, London

Cmnd 5012 (1972). *Report of the Committee on Privacy* (Chairman, The Rt Hon K. Younger), HMSO, London

Cmnd 6353 (1975). *Computers and Privacy*, HMSO, London
Cmnd 6732 (1977). *Copyright and Design Law*, HMSO, London
Cmnd 7341 (1978). *Report of the Committee on Data Protection* (Chairman, Sir N. Lindop), HMSO, London.
Cmnd 8302 (1981). *The Reform of the Law Relating to Copyright*, HMSO, London
Conway, R.W., Maxwell, W.L. and Morgan, H.L. (1972). On the implementation of security measures in information systems. *Communications of ACM*, Vol. 15, No. 4, 211–20
Cornish, W.R. (1981). *Intellectual Property: Patents, Copyright, Trade Marks and Allied Rights*, Sweet and Maxwell, London
Court, J.M. (1984). *Personal Data Protection – The 1984 Act and its implications*, NCC, Manchester
Courtney, R.H. (1977). Security risk assessment in electronic data processing systems. *AFIPS Conference Proceedings, NCC*, Vol. 46, 97–104
Datapro (1985). *Computer Weekly/Datapro Survey – British User Ratings of Computer Systems*, Datapro, CH-1164, Burchillon, Switzerland
Davis, K.W. and Perry. W.E. (1982). *Auditing Computer Applications*, Wiley, New York
Deloitte, Haskins and Sells (1982). *The External Auditor as Privacy Inspector*, NCC, Manchester
Denning, D.E.R. (1982). *Cryptography and Data Security*, Addison-Wesley, Reading, Massachusetts
Denning, D.E.R. and Denning, P.J. (1977). Certification of programs for secure information flow. *Communications of ACM*, Vol. 20, No. 7, 504–13
Denning, D.E.R. and Denning, P.J. (1979). Data security. *ACM Computing Surveys*, Vol. 11, No. 3, 227–49
Diffie, W. and Hellman, M.E. (1976). New directions in cryptography. *IEEE Transactions on Information Theory*, Vol. 11, No. 22, 644–54
Diffie, W. and Hellman, M.E. (1977). Exhaustive cryptanalysis of the NBS data encryption standard. *Computer*, Vol. 10, No. 6, 74–84
Dobkin, D., Jones, A.K. and Lipton, R.J. (1976). *Secure Databases: Protection against User Inference*, Research Report 65, Department of Computer Science, Yale University, New Haven, Connecticut
Enticknap, N. (1982). Patent granted after ten year legal tussle. *Computer Weekly*, 29 July, 6
Farquhar, W. and Wong, K.K. (1983). *Computer Crime Casebook*, BIS Applied Systems, London
Fenton, J.S. (1974). Memoryless subsystems. *Computer Journal*, Vol. 17, No. 2, 143–7
Fernandez, E.B., Summers, R.C. and Wood, C. (1981). *Database Security and Integrity*, Addison-Wesley, Reading, Massachusetts
FIPS 31 (1974). *Guidelines for Automatic Data Processing, Physical Security and Risk Management*, FIPS PUB 31, National Bureau of Standards, Washington, DC
FIPS 46 (1977). *Data Encryption Standard*, FIPS PUB 46, National Bureau of Standards, Washington, DC
FIPS 65 (1979). *Guidelines for Automated Data Processing Risk Analysis*, FIPS PUB 65, National Bureau of Standards, Washington, DC
FIPS 73 (1980). *Guidelines for Security of Computer Applications*, FIPS PUB 73, National Bureau of Standards, Washington, DC
Franz, C.R., Wilkins, S.J. and Bower, J.C. (1981). A critical review of proprietary software protection. *Information and Management*, Vol. 4, 55–69

Friedman, S. (1982). Contingency and disaster planning. *Computers and Security*, Vol. 1, No. 1, 34–40

Gaines, R.S. and Shapiro, N.Z. (1978). Some security principles and their application to computer security. *Operating Systems Review*, Vol. 12, No. 3, 19–28

Gilhooley, I.A. (1980). Data security. In *Advances in Computer Security Management, Vol. 1* (ed. T.A. Rullo), Heyden, London, 33–56

Glaseman, S., Turn, R., and Gaines, R.S. (1977). Problem areas in computer security assessment. *AFIPS Conference Proceedings, NCC*, Vol. 46, 105–12

Goldstein, R.C. (1975). The costs of privacy. *Datamation*, Vol. 21, No. 10, 65–9

Gostin, L. (1984). *The Data Protection Bill – an NCCL briefing*, National Council for Civil Liberties, London

Graham R.L. (1984). The legal protection of computer software. *Communications of ACM*, Vol. 27, No. 5, 422–6

Grover, D.J. and Hart, R.J. (1982). Computing and reform of copyright protection. *Computer Bulletin*, Vol. II, No. 31, 4–5

Harrison, M.A., Ruzzo, W.L. and Ullman, J.D. (1976). Protection in operating systems. *Communications of ACM*, Vol. 19, No. 8, 461–71

Hartson, R. and Hsaio, D.K. (1975). *Languages for Specifying Protection Requirements in Database Systems (Part 1)*, Report OSU-CISRC-TR-74-10, Ohio State University, Computer and Information Science Research Center, Columbus, Ohio

Hayhurst, W. (1982). Pythagoras and the computer. *EIPR*, Vol. 8, 223–7

Highland, H.J. (1983). Impact of microcomputers on total computer security. *Proceedings of IFIP Security Conference*, North-Holland, Amsterdam, 119–29

Hoffman, L.J. (1977). *Modern Methods for Computer Security and Privacy*, Prentice-Hall, Englewood Cliffs, New Jersey

Hoffman, L.J. (1980). *Computers and Privacy in the Next Decade*, Academic Press, New York

Hoffman, L.J. and Miller, W.F. (1970). Getting a personal dossier from a statistical data bank. *Datamation*, Vol. 16, No. 5, 74–5

Hoffman, L.J., Michelman, E.H. and Clements, D. (1978). Securate – security evaluation and analysis using fuzzy metrics. *AFIPS Conference Proceedings, NCC*, Vol. 47, 531–40

Hsiao, D.K., Kerr, D.S. and Madnick, S.E. (1979). *Computer Security*, Academic Press, New York

IBM (1974). *Data Security and Data Processing, Volume 3, Part 1, State of Illinois: Executive Overview*, G320-1372-0, IBM, New York

IBM (1976). *Data Security Controls and Procedures – a Philosophy for DP Installations*, G320-5649-00, IBM, New York

Kahn, D. (1967). *The Codebreakers*, Macmillan, New York

Kimmance, P.F. (1981). *Computer Fraud Survey*, Local Government Audit Inspectorate, London

Kline, C.S. and Popek, G.J. (1979). Public key versus conventional key encryption. *AFIPS Conference Proceedings, NCC*, Vol. 48, 831–8

Lampson, B.W. (1971). Protection. *Proceedings of Information Science and Systems*, 437–43

Land, F.F. (1982). Tutorial on participative design. *Computer Journal*, Vol. 25, No. 2, 283–5

Lane, V.P. and Corcoran, J.B. (1978). Systems from conception to successful implementation in the office. *Proceedings of CAD 1978 Conference*, IPC, Sutton

Lane, V.P. and Step. J. (1985). The formidable if not insurmountable organisational problems of disaster recovery planning. *IFIP Security 1985 Conference Proceedings*, North-Holland, Amsterdam

Lane, V.P. and Wright, F.G. (1979). Human resources systematically applied to ensure computer security. *Proceedings of 2nd European Conference on Informatics, held in Venice*, Springer, Berlin

Lennon, R.E. (1978). Cryptography architecture for information security. *IBM Systems Journal*, Vol. 17, No. 2, 138–51

Linden, T.A. (1975). Operating system structures to support security and reliable software. *ACM Computing Surveys*, Vol. 8, No. 4, 409–45

Linowes, D.F. (1977). *Personal Privacy in an Information Society; the Report of the Privacy Protection Study Commission*, GPO Catalog No. Y3, P93/5.1

Lobel, J. (1980). Risk analysis in the 1980s. *AFIPS Conference Proceedings, NCC*, Vol. 49, 831–6

Loeckx, J. and Sieber, K. (1984). *The Foundations of Program Verification*, Wiley, Chichester

Martin, J. (1973). *Security, Accuracy and Privacy in Computer Systems*, Prentice-Hall, Englewood Cliffs, New Jersey

Martin, J. (1976). *Systems Performance: Human Factors and Systems Failures – Engineering Reliability Techniques*, Open University, Milton Keynes, 12–20

Maude, T. and Maude, D. (1984). Hardware protection against software piracy. *Communications of ACM*, Vol. 27, No. 9, 950–9

McLening, M. (1983). The software protection racket. *Software*, Vol. 2, No. 6, 4–12

McNulty, L. (1980). The Federal Aviation Administration computer security program. In *Advances in Computer Security Management, Vol. 1* (ed. T.A. Rullo), Heyden, London 231–45

McPhee, W.S. (1974). Operating system integrity in OS/VS2. *IBM Systems Journal*, Vol. 13, No. 3, 230–52

Miller, A.R., (1971). *Assault on Privacy*, University of Michigan Press, Ann Arbor, Michigan

Mooers, C.N. (1975). Computer software and copyright. *ACM Computing Surveys*, Vol. 7, No. 1, 45–73

Norback, C.T. (1981). *The Computer Invasion – What Information They Have on You*, Von Nostrand Reinhold, New York

Norman, A.R.D. (1983). *Computer Insecurity*, Chapman and Hall, London

Page-Jones, M. (1980). *The Practical Guide to Structured Systems Design*, Yourdon Press, New York

Parker, D.B. (1981). *Computer Security Management*, Reston Publishing, Reston, Virginia

Parker, D.B. and Madden, J.D. (1978). *ADP Occupational Vulnerabilities*, SRI International, Menlo Park, California

Parker, D.B., Nycum, S.H. and Ware, W.H. (1984). Computers crime and privacy – a national dilemma: Congressional testimony from industry. *Communications of ACM*, Vol. 27, No. 4, 312–21

Perry, W.E. (1981). *Computer Control and Security*, Wiley, New York

Peterson, J. and Silberschatz, A. (1982). *Operating System Concepts*, Addison-Wesley, Reading, Massachusetts

Reed, S.K. (1977). *Automatic Data Processing Risk Assessment*, NBS IR 77-1228, National Bureau of Standards, Washington, DC

Rivest, R.L., Shamir, A. and Adleman, L. (1978). A method for obtaining digital signatures and public-key cryptosystems. *Communications of ACM*, Vol. 21, No. 2, 120–6

Rodriguez, J.J. and Fisher, P.S. (1980). Security problems in a database environment. In *Advances in Computer Security Management, Vol. 1* (ed. T.A. Rullo), Heyden, London, 122–39

Ruder, B. and Madden, J.D. (1978). *An Analysis of Computer Security Safeguards for Detecting and Preventing Computer Misuse*, NBS SP 500-25, National Bureau of Standards, Washington, DC

Rule, J.B. (1974). *Private Lives and Public Surveillance*, Allen Lane, Penguin, London

Saltzer, J.H. and Schroeder, M.D. (1975). The protection of information in computer systems. *Proc. IEEE*, Vol. 63, No. 9, 1278–308

Samocuik, M. (1982). Corporate attitudes to computer misuse; a case study. *Computer Fraud and Security Bulletin*, Vol. 4, No. 7, 1–27

Scharf, J.D. (1980). Department of Defence network security considerations. In *Advances in Computer Security Management, Vol. 1* (ed. T.A. Rullo), Heyden, London, 202–30

Schlorer, J. (1975). Identification and retrieval of personal records from a statistical data bank. *Methods of Information in Medicine*, Vol. 14, No. 1, 7–13

Schlorer, J. (1979). *Disclosure from Statistical Databases: Quantitative Aspects of Trackers*, Inst. Medizinische Statistik und Dokumentation, University Glessen, West Germany

Schweitzer, J.A. (1982). *Managing Information Security: a Program for the Electronic Information Age*, Butterworth, London

Shannon, C.E. (1951). Prediction and entrophy of printed English. *Bell System Technical Journal*, 50–64

Simmons, G.J. (1979). Symmetric and asymmetric encryption. *ACM Computing Surveys*, Vol. 11, No. 4, 305–30

Simons, G.L. (1982). *Privacy in the Computer Age*, NCC, Manchester

Smith, J.E. (1980). Risk management for small computer installations. In *Advances in Computer Security Management*, Vol. 1 (Ed. T.A. Rullo), Heyden, London, 1–32

Snyder, L. (1981). Formal models of capability based protection systems. *IEEE Transactions on Computers*, Vol. C30, No. 3, 172–81

Spear, R. (1976). *Systems Performance: Human Factors and Systems Failures – the Hixon Analysis*, Open University, Milton Keynes

Squires, T. (1980). *Computer Security – the Personnel Aspect*, NCC, Manchester

Squires, T. (1981). *Security in Systems Design*, NCC, Manchester

Stern, R.H. (1978). Protection of computer programs, Parker v Flook. *EIPR*, vol. 1, 37–8

Stern, R.H. (1982). The case of the purloined object code: can it be solved? Part 1: The problems. *Byte*, September, 420–39

Sullivan, R. (1982). Europeans devise rapid method to determine if number is prime. *New York Times*, 5 February, A.16

Tapper, C. (1982). *Computer Law*, 2nd edition, Longman, Harlow

Ware, W.H. (1973). *Records, Computers and the Rights of Citizens*, US Government Printing Office, Washington, DC

Waring, L.P. (1978). *Management Handbook of Computer Security*, NCC, Manchester

Watne, D.A. and Turney, P.B.B. (1984). *Auditing EDP Systems*, Prentice-Hall, Englewood Cliffs, New Jersey

Watson, L. (1984). *A Systems Approach to Failures – Complexity, Management and Change*, Open University, Milton Keynes

Weissman, C. (1969). Security controls in the adept-50 time-sharing system. *Proceedings AFIPS Fall Jt Computer Conference*, Vol. 35, 119–33

Weissman, C. (1975). Secure computer operation with virtual machine partitioning. *AFIPS Conference, Proceedings NCC*, Vol. 44, 929–34

Westin, A. (1972). *Databanks in a Free Society: Computers, Record-keeping and Privacy*, Quadrangle Books, New York

WIPO (1978). *Model Provisions on the Protection of Computer Software*, Publication No. 814(E), International Bureau of the World Intellectual Property Organisation, Geneva

Wong, K.K. (1977). *Computer Security – Risk Analysis and Control*, NCC, Manchester

Wong, K.K. (1984). Data protection law. *Data Processing*, Vol. 26, No. 1, 34–7

Wood, H.M. (1977). The use of passwords for controlling access to remote computer systems and services. *AFIPS Conference, Proceedings NCC*, Vol. 46, 27–33

Wood, H.M. (1980). Computer based password techniques. In *Advances in Computer Security Management, Vol. 1* (ed. T.A. Rullo), Heyden, London, 141–67

Woodward, F. and Hoffman, L.J. (1974). Worst case costs for dynamic data element security decisions. *Proceedings ACM Conference*, 539–44

Index